# THE MATHEMATICS PLAYBOOK

# THE MATHEMATICS PLAYBOOK

## Implementing What Works Best in the Classroom

**JOHN ALMARODE**
**KATERI THUNDER**
**MICHELLE SHIN**
**DOUGLAS FISHER**
**NANCY FREY**

FOR INFORMATION:

Corwin
A SAGE Company
2455 Teller Road
Thousand Oaks, California 91320
(800) 233-9936
www.corwin.com

SAGE Publications Ltd.
1 Oliver's Yard
55 City Road
London EC1Y 1SP
United Kingdom

SAGE Publications India Pvt. Ltd.
Unit No 323-333, Third Floor, F-Block
International Trade Tower Nehru Place
New Delhi 110 019
India

SAGE Publications Asia-Pacific Pte. Ltd.
18 Cross Street #10-10/11/12
China Square Central
Singapore 048423

Vice President and
 Editorial Director:   Monica Eckman
Publisher:  Jessica Allan
Content Development Editor:   Mia Rodriguez
Senior Editorial Assistant:   Natalie Delpino
Production Editor:   Tori Mirsadjadi
Copy Editor:   Sheree Van Vreede
Typesetter:   C&M Digitals (P) Ltd.
Proofreader:   Jennifer Grubba
Indexer:   Integra
Cover Designer:   Gail Buschman
Marketing Manager:   Olivia Bartlett

Library of Congress Cataloging-in-Publication Data

Names: Almarode, John, author. | Thunder, Kateri, author. | Shin, Michelle, author. | Fisher, Douglas, 1965- author. | Frey, Nancy, 1959- author.

Title: The Mathematics Playbook : Implementing What Works Best in the Classroom / John Almarode, Kateri Thunder, Michelle Shin, Douglas FIsher, Nancy Frey.

Description: Thousand Oaks, California : Corwin, [2024] | Includes bibliographical references and index.

Identifiers: LCCN 2023046567 | ISBN 9781071907658 (spiral bound) | ISBN 9781071907665 (epub) | ISBN 9781071907672 (epub) | ISBN 9781071907689 (pdf)

Subjects: LCSH: Mathematics—Study and teaching.

Classification: LCC QA135.6 .A36 2024 | DDC 510.71—dc23/eng/20231214
LC record available at https://lccn.loc.gov/2023046567

This book is printed on acid-free paper.

24 25 26 27 28 10 9 8 7 6 5 4 3 2 1

# Contents

Visit the companion website at
**resources.corwin.com/themathematicsplaybook**
for downloadable resources.

**Note From the Publisher:** The authors have provided web content in the book that is available to you through QR (quick response) codes. To read a QR code, you must have a smartphone or tablet with a camera. We recommend that you download a QR code reader app made specifically for your phone or tablet brand.

**The links may also be accessed at resources.corwin.com/themathematicsplaybook**

# About the Authors

John Almarode, PhD, is a professor of education at James Madison University. He was awarded the inaugural Sarah Miller Luck Endowed Professorship in 2015 and received an Outstanding Faculty Award from the State Council for Higher Education in Virginia in 2021. In 2022–2023, John was named a Madison Scholar in the College of Education. Before his academic career, John started as a mathematics and science teacher in Augusta County, Virginia. As an author, John has written multiple educational books focusing on science and mathematics, and he has co-created a new framework for developing, implementing, and sustaining professional learning communities called PLC+. His collaborative work with colleagues on what works best in teaching and learning includes *How Tutoring Works, Visible Learning in Early Childhood, How Learning Works, How Feedback Works,* and *How Scaffolding Works.*

Kateri Thunder, PhD, has the pleasure of collaborating with learners and educators from school divisions and early learning centers around the world to translate research into practice. She has served as an inclusive early childhood educator, an Upward Bound educator, a mathematics specialist, an assistant professor of mathematics education at James Madison University, and site director for the Central Virginia Writing Project. Her research, writing, and presentations focus on equity and access in early childhood and mathematics education, as well as on the intersection of literacy and mathematics for teaching and learning. Kateri has co-authored *Teaching Mathematics in the Visible Learning Classroom Series*, *The Success Criteria Playbook*, *Visible Learning in Early Childhood*, and *The Early Childhood Education Playbook*.

**Michelle Shin, EdD,** is an educational leader who brings more than 15 years of experience and research to this role. She served as a classroom teacher in mathematics and as a site administrator in San Diego, California. She attended the University of California, San Diego, and received a bachelor's degree in mathematics/secondary education and a master's degree in education. She also attended San Diego State University, where she wrote her dissertation, "Trust: An Essential Focus for Effective Leadership," and earned a doctoral degree in educational leadership in PreK to 12.

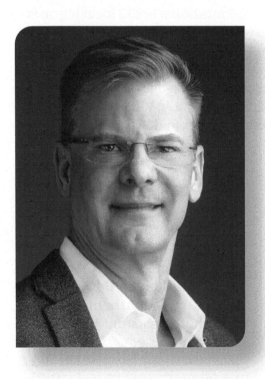

**Douglas Fisher, PhD,** is professor and chair of educational leadership at San Diego State University, where he teaches quantitative methods and instructional leadership courses. Doug is also a teacher leader at Health Sciences High and Middle College. Previously, Doug was an early intervention teacher and elementary school educator. He has published numerous articles on teaching and learning, as well as books such as *The Teacher Clarity Playbook*; *PLC+*; *Visible Learning for Mathematics*; *Comprehension: The Skill, Will, and Thrill of Reading*; *How Tutoring Works*; and *How Learning Works*.

Nancy Frey, PhD, is a professor in educational leadership at San Diego State University and a teacher leader at Health Sciences High and Middle College. Her published titles include *Visible Learning in Mathematics*, *Leader Credibility*, *How Feedback Works*, and *The Teacher Clarity Playbook*. Nancy is a credentialed special educator, reading specialist, and administrator in California and learns from teachers and students every day.

# Introduction

This playbook is about teaching and learning mathematics. Yes, mathematics. Given that we will focus on mathematics, it seems appropriate to start with math.

1. Think of any number, and write it down here: _____.

2. Multiply that number by 3 (you can use a calculator). Write that answer here: _____.

3. Add 45 to the result. Again, calculators are permitted. Answer: _____.

4. Double the answer in #3. Answer: _____.

5. Take your answer from #4 and divide that number by 6. Answer: _____.

6. Subtract your original number (see #1) from the answer in #5. Answer: _____.

Circle your final answer in #6. Hold on to this final number. We will come back and visit this task in just a moment.

This Playbook is not just focused on the content, skills, procedures, conceptual understandings, and application of mathematics, but it is also focused on the teaching and learning of mathematics in our schools and classrooms. From counting to conic sections, patterns to permutations, radii to rational equations, and fractions to fractals, the questions we aim to answer include:

- How do we foster, nurture, and sustain mathematics learning?

- How do we approach the teaching and learning of mathematics to ensure all learners have equity of access and opportunity to the highest level of mathematics learning possible?

- What are the non-negotiables in a high-quality mathematics task?

- How do we know if learners really "get it"? These are the questions we strive to address in this Playbook.

However, these are likely not the only questions you have about your classroom or your students. They certainly are not the only questions we have about mathematics teaching and learning. Within the daily hustle and bustle in our classrooms, we come face to face with many celebrations and challenges. Those celebrations and challenges likely lead you to this Playbook. As a former high school mathematics teacher, John wondered why learners engaged in mathematics tasks while in class but did not see the value of practice in moving their learning forward. He also enjoyed celebrating moments when learners demonstrated their knowledge, skills, and understanding around, say, linear equations, but he was challenged when that knowledge, those skills, or the understandings did not transfer to different contexts. What celebrations and challenges do you experience in your mathematics teaching and your students' mathematics learning?

Reflect on your mathematics teaching and your students' mathematics learning. What questions come to mind? Jot these questions down in the space below so that we can revisit them throughout our work in this Playbook.

Throughout the modules in this Playbook, we will pull together the latest research on what works best and explore the implications of that research on mathematics teaching and learning.

## OUR LEARNING INTENTION

We are learning about what works best in mathematics teaching and learning, so that we can implement these ideas, approaches, strategies, and interventions in our classrooms.

However, this goal should not be interpreted to mean that the modules and tasks within this Playbook provide a step-by-step recipe that guarantees students will learn. The purpose of this Playbook is to take a closer look at the creation and implementation of mathematics learning experiences so that we can foster, nurture, and sustain mathematics learning for all our learners. The potential to maximize student learning in mathematics can only be actualized through effective implementation. The modules of this Playbook focus on expanding our understanding of what that looks like in our classrooms and how we can better use what we know about how students learn. In addition, we will explore how to better engage our learners to self-monitor, self-reflect, and self-evaluate their mathematics learning.

> Return to the previous questions you generated about your mathematics teaching and your students' mathematics learning. Take some time and revise those questions into your learning goals for this Playbook. If you are working with your professional learning community (PLC+) team, your grade-level planning team, or your fellow mathematics teachers, develop a shared list of goals.

## THE LEARNING PLAN WITHIN THE MODULES

This is a Playbook, which by definition, then, contains a collection of tactics and methods used by a team to accomplish a common goal and get things done (Merriam-Webster, 2023). In the case of this Playbook, the learning intention is to understand what works best in mathematics teaching and learning, so that we can implement these ideas, approaches, strategies, and interventions into our classrooms. Therefore, each of the subsequent modules is designed to support your thinking and decision-making around mathematics teaching and learning in your classroom. But the modules are not necessarily intended to be completed in sequential order or all at once. When athletic coaches and their teams use playbooks to get things done (e.g., score a goal in soccer, score a run in a cricket match, score a touchdown in American football), they select the plays that best fit the *current context or situation*. Likewise, the modules in this Playbook should be used by your team when the current context or situation calls for the module. So, what's the plan?

This Playbook is divided into four parts (Table I.1). The first section of modules will identify and define the elements or strands of mathematics teaching and learning: procedural knowledge, conceptual understanding, and the application of concepts and thinking. Together, we will analyze standards and curricular documents to ensure we integrate all strands of mathematics proficiency into our instruction. This also reflects one of our foundational beliefs underlying this Playbook and our first big idea: Our perspective on mathematics teaching and learning has been far too narrow.

## BIG IDEA #1

Mathematics teaching must integrate all aspects of "what it means to learn mathematics."

When we broaden our perspective on what is meant by mathematics learning, our teaching broadens the pathways for learners to engage, represent, and demonstrate their mathematics learning.

## ACTIVATING PRIOR KNOWLEDGE

In the space provided, jot down what you think is meant by the statement, *mathematics teaching must integrate all aspects of "what it means to learn mathematics."* What do you think is meant by procedural knowledge, conceptual knowledge, and application of concepts and thinking? We will come back and revise your responses later in this Playbook, if necessary.

The second part of this Playbook focuses on how we translate and communicate mathematics learning to your students. We will spend time thinking about learning and engagement in our mathematics classrooms and what it means to be a good mathematics learner. Both learning and engagement are highly contextualized and will require us to self-reflect on our expectations and then what is communicated to our students.

## BIG IDEA #2

The expectations for mathematics learning must be clearly shared with and communicated to our learners.

When students know what they are learning and what successful learning looks like, they are more likely to engage in the learning tasks. However, there are chokepoints, barriers, and pitfalls in learning and engagement. These barriers, as we have discovered in our own work, result in frustration and unproductive struggle. Awareness of these chokepoints to learning, barriers to engagement, and pitfalls in teaching will allow us to proactively adjust our thinking and decision making around mathematics teaching and learning in our classrooms.

### ACTIVATING PRIOR KNOWLEDGE

In the space provided, jot down how you share and communicate about the learning in your mathematics classroom. What are barriers, chokepoints, and pitfalls to learning and engagement that you have already identified in your classroom? Again, we will return to your responses later in this Playbook.

Oh, one quick and final comment about this second part of the Playbook. Did you notice that learning was listed before engagement? That is on purpose. Circle, highlight, or underline the three times *learning and engagement* are listed together in the above paragraph. We will explain the significance of the pairing and the specific order of the pairing at the start of the second part of this Playbook.

The third part of this Playbook takes an up-close look at the design and implementation of mathematics experiences and tasks.

# BIG IDEA #3

Mathematics teaching and learning must be reflected in rigorous mathematical experiences and tasks.

By the time we arrive at this part of the Playbook, whether you start your journey here or have worked your way through the previous modules, this is where the "rubber meets the road." Together, we will take a close-up look at the specific experiences and tasks we design and implement in our classrooms. What are the characteristics of rigorous mathematics tasks? This includes infusing more discussion, dialogue, and talk into mathematics learning. Consistently quiet mathematics classrooms are mathematics classrooms in which learning is compromised.

Furthermore, how do we scaffold those tasks to ensure all learners have access to the highest level of learning possible? If you flip back to p. 2, one question you may have generated was about the "readiness" of certain learners for specific content, skills, and understandings. How do we support learners that are not ready, YET? Part three of this Playbook will investigate how to scaffold a mathematics experience or task so that all learners make progress toward the learning goal. The emphasis here will be that all learners are working toward the same learning outcomes. Their path toward those outcomes may look different from their peers.

We will close out this third part of the Playbook by addressing the "pink gorilla" in the room: practice. How do we help learners see the value in practice? Not just any practice, but practice that moves mathematics learning forward.

## ACTIVATING PRIOR KNOWLEDGE

In the space provided, describe a mathematics experience or task that you felt was VERY successful in your classroom. Then describe a mathematics experience or task that was a complete disaster. No judgment, we've all been there. How are these two episodes similar? How are they different? We come back to this response when we get to Part 3 of this Playbook.

From there, we enter the final part of this Playbook. This final part focuses on the role of generating visible evidence of and for mathematics learning.

## BIG IDEA #4

Mathematics teaching and learning requires the generation and interpretation of evidence.

We will look at the value in making student thinking visible so that we can answer the question "Where to next?" One specific module looks at ways to interpret the evidence our learners generate and make purposeful, intentional, and deliberate decisions about where to go next in mathematics teaching and learning. We spend so much time on "data" but very little time on what to do with that data! This Playbook aims to rectify this problem. Finally, we will devote considerable attention to the role of self-monitoring, self-reflection, and self-evaluation through effective feedback in developing self-regulated mathematics learners. These learners know what to do, when they don't know what to do, and we are no longer their math teachers.

TABLE I.1 ● The Mathematics Playbook overview.

| PART 1 | |
| --- | --- |
| Module 1 | What are the elements of mathematics teaching and learning? |
| Module 2 | How do I identify the elements of mathematics teaching and learning for my classroom? |
| Module 3 | How do I evaluate the inclusion of all aspects of mathematics teaching and learning into my classroom? |
| **PART 2** | |
| Module 4 | What is a mathematics learner, and what makes a mathematics learner in my classroom? |
| Module 5 | What is an *engaged* mathematics learner? |
| Module 6 | What are the misalignments, misconceptions, and missed opportunities in mathematical learning and engagement? |
| **PART 3** | |
| Module 7 | What are the characteristics of a rigorous mathematics task? |
| Module 8 | How do I facilitate Math Talk in my classroom? |
| Module 9 | How do I implement worked examples into my classroom? |
| Module 10 | How do I scaffold mathematics tasks in my classroom? |
| Module 11 | How do I integrate deliberate practice into my classroom? |

*(Continued)*

(Continued)

| PART 4 | |
| --- | --- |
| Module 12 | How do I generate evidence of and for learning in my classroom? |
| Module 13 | How do I notice the evidence in my classroom? |
| Module 14 | What is the role of feedback in my classroom? |
| Module 15 | How do I develop self-regulated learners? |

## LEARNING WITHIN THE MODULES

We make two assumptions about your learning journey in this Playbook. First, you are an educator, whether that be a preservice teacher, an instructional assistant, teacher, teacher leader, instructional coach, or curriculum specialist that has or will have a direct connection to mathematics teaching and learning. Second, we assume that you have noticed that your learners, and maybe even you, seek to enhance the learning of your students in mathematics. You may be prompted by data suggesting areas of growth or opportunity in your professional practice. You may be motivated simply because you have set this as a professional goal and are looking to refresh, rejuvenate, or revive your mathematics teaching and your students' learning. Or you may be motivated because you are not as comfortable or confident in your mathematics teaching. If these assumptions fit your current professional learning journey, this Playbook is for you.

Each module begins with a self-assessment and then introduces a specific goal, an explanation of the ideas within the module to establish the focus for the learning (a learning intention). The module then continues with modeling how to take the research and translate the findings into the reality of your specific school or classroom. There will be many examples across all grade levels. Examples will cover primary, elementary, middle school, and high school content, skills, practices, dispositions, and understandings. We seek to provide a wide range of examples to show that what works best in mathematics teaching and learning, as well as works best across all grade levels.

Each module offers you an opportunity for practice and application with a variety of concepts, skills, understandings, and grade levels. The practice section encourages you to write your answers and discuss them with your team, if possible. Although using this book as part of your personal learning is possible, creating and implementing what works best in mathematics is best done collectively with colleagues. One benefit of this collaboration is the opportunity to engage in critical dialogue regarding what this looks like for you and your learners. These critical conversations will provide feedback on your professional learning journey.

# COLLABORATING TO CREATE AND IMPLEMENT HIGH-QUALITY SUCCESS CRITERIA

The most effective way to create and implement mathematics learning experiences so that we can foster, nurture, and sustain mathematics learning for all our learners is to work collaboratively with your grade-level team, mathematics department, or PLC+. We believe that the work of this Playbook is an essential component of the work you do in your PLC+. The use of these five guiding questions of PLC+ will keep the focus relentlessly on the learning of our students:

- Where are we going?

- Where are we now?

- How do we move learning forward?

- What did we learn today?

- Who benefited and who did not benefit? (Fisher et al., 2020, p. 8)

In PLC+, teachers identify learning outcomes and discuss ideas for mathematics instruction. They meet to review student work and figure out if their efforts have been fruitful. They also talk about students who need additional scaffolding to be successful. This discussion is all informed and supported by rigorous mathematics tasks. We must ensure that we all have high expectations, focus on a common understanding of what learning and engagement look like, activate the conversation around learning, and ensure equity of access and opportunity to learning for all students (Table I.2).

**TABLE I.2** ● How the Mathematics Playbook supports the work of PLC+.

| PLC QUESTION | MATHEMATICS PLAYBOOK MODULE |
|---|---|
| Where are we going? | Module 1: What are the elements of mathematics teaching and learning? |
| | Module 2: How do I identify the elements of mathematics teaching and learning for my classroom? |
| | Module 4: What is a mathematics learner, and what makes a mathematics learner in my classroom? |
| | Module 15: How do I develop self-regulated mathematics learners? |
| Where are we now? | Module 3: How do I evaluate the inclusion of all aspects of mathematics teaching and learning into my classroom? |

*(Continued)*

(Continued)

| PLC QUESTION | MATHEMATICS PLAYBOOK MODULE |
|---|---|
| How do we move learning forward? | Module 5: What is an *engaged* mathematics learner? |
| | Module 6: What are the misalignments, misconceptions, and missed opportunities in mathematical learning and engagement? |
| | Module 7: What are the characteristics of a rigorous mathematics task? |
| | Module 8: How do I facilitate Math Talk in my classroom? |
| | Module 9: How do I implement worked examples into my classroom? |
| | Module 11: How do I integrate deliberate practice into my classroom? |
| What did we learn today? | Module 12: How do I generate evidence of and for learning in my classroom? |
| | Module 13: How do I notice the evidence in my classroom? |
| | Module 14: What is the role of feedback in my classroom? |
| Who benefited and who did not benefit? | Module 10: How do I scaffold mathematics tasks in my classroom? |

online resources ⤵ This resource is available for download at **resources.corwin.com/themathematicsplaybook**.

Before we close, flip back to the initial mathematics task in this module. Was your final answer 15? Go ahead, try different numbers to see if you always arrive at 15. Amazing, right? This initial task serves as a metaphor for our learning journey in this Playbook. Regardless of your initial number, the specific numeric operations will lead you to the final answer of 15. The numeric operations or decisions in this initial task mathematically change your starting number to 15. Likewise, regardless of the initial starting point of our learners, their encounters and experiences in our schools and classrooms have the potential to have a positive effect on their mathematics learning. They allow all learners the access and opportunity for successful mathematics learning. Just like the initial mathematics task in this module, these encounters and these experiences are purposeful, intentional, and deliberate. They are by design, not by chance. That is the power we have as mathematics teachers. That is the hope we have as mathematics educators. What follows in these modules, across the pages of this Playbook, is a close-up look at the decisions we make each and every day to ensure that our students have a great mathematics teacher, not by chance but by design.

Now, let's get started!

# What Are the Essential Elements of Mathematics Teaching and Learning?

Without any delay, let's dive into a few mathematics problems. Of course, you are not obligated to do all of them, but working through the following three problems will certainly frame our work in this module.

1. Subtract: $\frac{9}{10} - \frac{2}{5}$. Write your answer in simplest form. Describe the steps you took to find the solution to this problem.

2. Describe how $\frac{1}{2} + \frac{1}{4}$ is solved differently from $\frac{1}{2} + \frac{1}{3}$.

3. Fernando has $\frac{7}{8}$ of a cup of apple cider vinegar. He uses $\frac{1}{2}$ cup to make salad dressing and $\frac{1}{4}$ cup to make gazpacho. How much apple cider vinegar does Fernando have left?

4. Michelle has started rating the quality of commercials during the World Cup using a scale of 1 to 10. Her ratings so far are: 7, 8, 9, 4, 8, 3, 9, 7, 4, 6, 9, 6, 6, 1, 9. Make a histogram of the data.

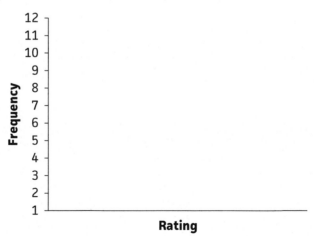

*(Continued)*

(Continued)

5. "Books by the Pound" is a used bookstore that offers one pound of books for $5.00.

   a. Graph the proportional relationship that gives the cost *y* in dollars of buying *x* pounds of books.

   b. Identify an ordered pair on the graph, and explain its meaning in the context of a bookstore purchase.

6. The migration pattern of a species of birds to different areas over the course of a year can be represented using the graph below. Create a table of *x*-values and *y*-values, and express whether the pattern follows a linear function. If the migratory pattern is linear, express how the constant change in *y* corresponds to a constant change in *x*.

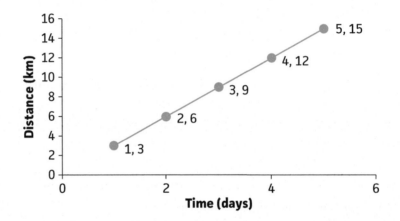

| X | Y |
| --- | --- |
| | |
| | |
| | |
| | |
| | |
| | |

7. Solve for *x* and *y*.

$9x - 2y = -5$

$-6x + y = -1$

8. The sum of two angles is 180 degrees. The difference between twice the larger angle and three times the smaller angle is 150 degrees. The following system of equations models this particular situation where *x* is the measure of the larger angle and *y* is the measure of the smaller angle. What is the measure of each angle?

$x + y = 180$

$2x - 3y = 150$

The purpose of these eight mathematics problems is not to test your mathematics knowledge, skills, and understandings. Instead, we want to immerse ourselves in mathematics learning to better grasp all aspects of "what it means to learn mathematics." This was our first big idea introduced in the Introduction. To solidify this big idea, please flip back to p. 4, grab that big idea, and rewrite it in the box below.

---

## BIG IDEA #1

Our mathematics teaching must . . . _____

_____ .

---

Much like a scatter plot, the various aspects of learning mathematics are scattered throughout those eight mathematics problems. Those aspects are identified by asking yourself what someone would have to know, understand, and be able to do to complete each problem. Now that you have solved these problems, let's analyze them through this new lens or perspective (see Table 1.1). As you engaged in each problem, what did you have to know, understand, and be able to do? Using the space provided, if possible, work collaboratively with your grade-level team, mathematics department, or professional learning community (PLC+) to make a list of the knowledge, understandings, and skills needed. We have provided a few examples to get you started.

| PROBLEM | WHAT DID YOU HAVE TO KNOW, UNDERSTAND, AND BE ABLE TO DO? |
|---|---|
| Subtract: $\frac{9}{10} - \frac{2}{5}$. Write your answer in simplest form. Describe the steps you took to find the solution to this problem. | *Example: must know what "simplest form" means* |
| Describe how $\frac{1}{2} + \frac{1}{4}$ is solved differently than $\frac{1}{2} + \frac{1}{3}$. | |
| Fernando has $\frac{7}{8}$ of a cup of apple cider vinegar. He uses $\frac{1}{2}$ cup to make salad dressing and $\frac{1}{4}$ cup to make gazpacho. How much apple cider vinegar does Fernando have left? | |
| Michelle has started rating the quality of commercials during the World Cup using a scale of 1 to 10. Her ratings so far are: 7, 8, 9, 4, 8, 3, 9, 7, 4, 6, 9, 6, 6, 1, 9. Make a histogram of the data. <br><br> *Frequency axis labeled 1–12, horizontal axis labeled Rating* | |
| "Books by the Pound" is a used bookstore that offers one pound of books for $5.00. <br> a. Graph the proportional relationship that gives the cost *y* in dollars of buying *x* pounds of books. <br> b. Identify an ordered pair on the graph and explain its meaning in the context of a bookstore purchase. | *Example: must understand the concept of an ordered pair* |

| PROBLEM | WHAT DID YOU HAVE TO KNOW, UNDERSTAND, AND BE ABLE TO DO? |
|---|---|
| The migration pattern of a species of birds to different areas over the course of a year can be represented using the graph below. Create a table of *x-values* and *y-values* and express whether the pattern follows a linear function. If the migratory pattern is linear, express how the constant change in *y* corresponds to a constant change in *x*. <br><br> Distance (km) vs Time (days) graph with points: 1, 3 / 2, 6 / 3, 9 / 4, 12 / 5, 15 | |
| Solve for *x* and *y*. <br><br> $9x - 2y = -5$ <br><br> $-6x + y = -1$ | *Example: must know the different ways/ procedures for solving a system of equations* |
| The sum of two angles is 180 degrees. The difference between twice the larger angle and three times the smaller angle is 150 degrees. The following system of equations models this particular situation where *x* is the measure of the larger angle and *y* is the measure of the smaller angle. What is the measure of each angle? <br><br> $x + y = 180$ <br><br> $2x - 3y = 150$ | |

Although this may come as no surprise to you, we still want to point out that this last exercise should highlight that learning mathematics involves more than just procedures, algorithms, and a series of steps to be followed by learners. What you and your colleagues added to the right column in Table 1.1 far exceeds the often emphasized plug-n-chug approach. If learning mathematics is more than just procedures, algorithms, and steps, then we must teach mathematics as more than just procedures, algorithms, and steps. This is the point of this initial module. Even though we can all say that there is more to mathematics teaching and learning than plug-n-chug, do we know what that "more" is? What are the elements of mathematics teaching and learning?

# MODULE #1

### Learning Intention

We are learning about the different elements of mathematics learning so that we can better integrate these elements into our mathematics teaching.

### Success Criteria

We'll know we've learned this when we can:

1. compare and contrast the different types of mathematics understanding.

2. identify the different elements of mathematics learning.

3. recognize these elements in standards and curriculum documents.

**Skemp's Article**

bit.ly/45Lmzy4

To read a QR code, you must have a smartphone or tablet with a camera. We recommend that you download a QR code reader app that is made specifically for your phone or tablet brand.

# UNDERSTANDING MATHEMATICS

To identify the elements of mathematics learning, let's take a look back at Skemp's article on understanding published in *Mathematics Teaching* in 1976. He considered mathematics understanding as a continuum between instrumental understanding and relational understanding.

Yes, we are actually referencing an article from the '70s. Before you tune us out, keep in mind that this seminal work is still relevant today. Flip back to the mathematics problems presented at the beginning of this module. To build our definition of instrumental understanding and relational understanding, let's compare and contrast problem #4 with problem #5 OR problem #7 with problem #8. The comparing and contrasting of these pairs of problems will help bring the end points of Skemp's continuum to life.

Use this Venn diagram to compare and contrast the pair of problems selected by you and your colleagues.

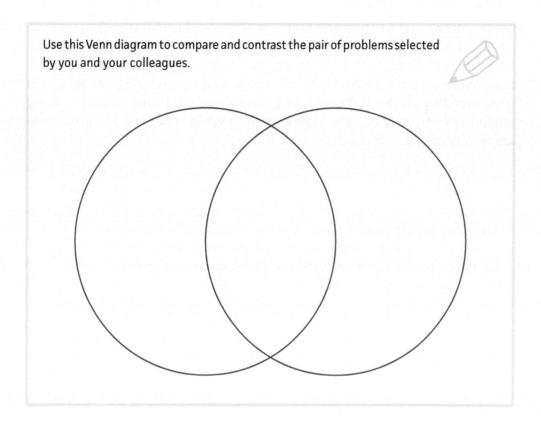

Skemp (1976) defined instrumental understanding as the type of understanding as rules without reasons. In other words, learners demonstrate instrumental understanding when they can solve a mathematics problem, invoke a specific procedure, utilize a certain algorithm, or check off a series of steps without knowing why. If you looked at problem #4 and problem #5, you may now notice that learners could simply plot the frequency of those ratings without knowing why they are doing it. However, in problem #5, they must understand the why so that they can explain the real-world context of an order pair in this particular problem. The same is true for problem #7 and problem #8. Going through procedure (e.g., elimination), algorithm (e.g., substitution), or steps (e.g., graphing) for solving systems of equations can be done without understanding why this leads us to a solution to a system of equations. What even is the solution to a system of equations? What does that mean?

Before moving to the other side of the continuum, take a moment and label the continuum below by writing *Instrumental Understanding* on the left side.

**Skemp's Continuum of Understanding**

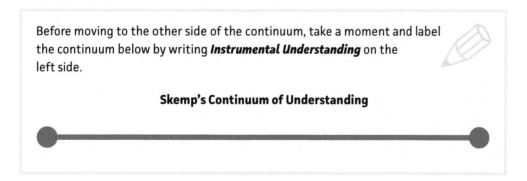

On the other end of the continuum is relational understanding. Skemp (1976) contrasted relational understanding with instrumental understanding in that relational understanding is the integration of both rules and reasons. Pause for a second and label the above continuum by placing *Relational Understanding* on the right side. Learners show relational understanding when they utilize a certain algorithm or engage in a series of steps and know why they are doing it.

---

Take a moment and use the space below to summarize your understanding of instrumental and relational understanding. In addition to your summaries, provide specific examples from your school or classroom.

_____

_____

_____

_____

---

Our guess is that every mathematics teacher, whether teaching kindergarten or calculus, wants students to learn mathematics to the level of relational understanding. Understanding the why behind what we do in mathematics is very important to the fostering, nurturing, and sustaining of mathematics learning. We all have examples of learners who struggled with mathematics concepts, skills, and understandings simply because their understanding of foundational ideas was purely instrumental. Problem #3 and problem #6 will likely create unproductive struggle and failure for learners that possess only an instrumental understanding of fractions and linear systems.

Most state standards in mathematics emphasize relational understanding either in the standard itself or in the curriculum frameworks or documents supporting those standards. With our new learning around instrumental and relational understanding, let's look at a specific standard to see where this is explicitly called out in these state-level documents. Take a look at the following statements extracted from a sixth-grade standard in the state of Georgia (Georgia Department of Education, 2021). This is not the full standard, nor are the following statements provided in the chart.

Using a highlighter or colorful writing utensil, identify where the statements from the standard indicate that learners must have relational understanding—rules WITH reason.

**PAR Standard 7**

bit.ly/49E0LHc

Link to the full sixth-grade standard on patterning and algebraic reasoning.

**Statement from the Sixth-Grade Patterning and Algebraic Reason (PAR) Standard 7. From the Georgia Department of Education (2021).**

1. Create practical, mathematical situations corresponding to specific inequalities.

2. Solve one-step equations and inequalities involving variables when values for the variables are given.

3. Solve an equation as a process of answering an authentic question, and explain their reasoning.

4. Explain that a variable can represent an unknown number or any number in a specified set.

5. Use concrete models or drawings and strategies based on place value, properties of operations, and/or the relationship between addition and subtraction and multiplication and division when solving one-step equations.

6. Explain why specific values from a specified set, if any, make the equation or inequality true.

7. Generate inequalities of the form $x > c, x > c, x < c$, or $x < c$ to explain situations that have infinitely many solutions.

8. Write one-step equations and inequalities to represent and solve problems.

9. Use substitution to determine whether a given number in a specified set makes an equation or inequality true.

10. Use of the symbols: $<, >, =, \leq$.

Which statements emphasize relational understanding? We would have highlighted statements 3, 4, and 6 because they align rules with reasoning, mathematical reasoning.

Moving forward in our teaching and in our students' learning, we must ensure we are aware that the understanding expected in our standards is essential for the following two reasons:

1. This helps us to ensure that we integrate all aspects of "what it means to learn mathematics."

2. When communicated to learners, helps them to have clarity about their mathematics learning.

We will devote a significant amount of time to that second reason in upcoming modules. For now, let's finally get to the aspects or elements of mathematics learning. The link between understanding and the elements of mathematics learning is as follows: Learners demonstrate understanding through various elements of mathematics learning.

# ELEMENTS OF MATHEMATICS UNDERSTANDING

Relational understanding is the synthesis of the elements of mathematics learning. Said differently, the interrelation of the elements of mathematics learning fosters, nurtures, and sustains relational understanding of mathematics. These elements, while they are associated with mathematics learning, are the result of encounters and experiences in our schools and classrooms. Ensuring that our schools and classrooms integrate all aspects of "what it means to learn mathematics," as well as allow all learners the access and opportunity to these elements, results in the amplification of mathematics learning. These aspects include conceptual knowledge, procedural fluency, strategic competence, adaptive reasoning, and productive dispositions. The integration of these aspects must be purposeful, intentional, and deliberate. Knowing and recognizing them in our standards and in our teaching is the first step to this integration by design.

*Conceptual Knowledge.* If you used any search engine and searched the words "conceptual knowledge," "conceptual learning," or "conceptual understanding," you would arrive at a significant number of definitions, descriptions, and explanations to review. In most cases, conceptual knowledge, conceptual learning, and conceptual understanding are loosely defined and described using very specific examples. For us, this leaves a lot of ambiguity about what is truly meant by this idea.

So, let's start with the basics. A concept is an abstract idea that serves as the fundamental building block for principles, thoughts, and beliefs (Goguen, 2005). In mathematics, we can think of concepts as mental representations of mathematical ideas such as part–whole, counting, addition, subtraction, multiplication, division, estimation, cardinality, space, and shape. E. Clark (1997) defined a concept as a big idea that helps make sense of, or connects, lots of ideas. Thus, conceptual knowledge is the relational understanding of these concepts in such a way that learners know the significance of the concept and how this concept is a part of specific content, skills, and understandings (see Table 1.2).

> Before moving forward, take a moment and connect relational understanding to conceptual knowledge. How are these ideas connected?
>
> _____
>
> _____
>
> _____
>
> _____

**TABLE 1.2** ● Relationship between concepts in mathematics and specific content, skills, and understandings.

| CONCEPT | RELATIONS TO SPECIFIC CONTENT, SKILLS, AND UNDERSTANDINGS |
|---|---|
| *Part-Whole* | • Composing and Decomposing Numbers<br>• Fractions<br>• Ratios and Proportions<br>• Sample and Population Statistics<br>• Permutations and Combinations |
| *Addition* | • Sum<br>• Patterns<br>• Multiplication (Repeated Addition)<br>• Number Lines<br>• Sequences and Series<br>• Matrix Algebra<br>• Principle of Superposition (Wave Theory) |
| *Cardinality* | • Counting<br>• Descriptive Statistics (e.g., frequencies)<br>• Relations and Functions<br>• Data Modelling<br>• Computer Programming<br>• Set Theory |

> Before moving to procedural fluency, let's take time to flip back to the sample standard on p. 18. Using a different highlighter or colorful writing utensil from the first task on p. 19, identify the concepts that students must understand to demonstrate proficiency in this specific standard. To get you started, we would highlight the concepts of equations, inequalities, and sets. Although those concepts are not the only ones, they should get you started on this task.

Once you and your colleagues have finished identifying the concepts, hang on to your answers from the previous tasks for use with subsequent tasks in this module. We are building to something and are laying the foundation by unpacking the elements of mathematics learning. Now, let's turn our attention to procedural fluency.

*Procedural Fluency.* If conceptual knowledge is all about big ideas, then procedural fluency is the knowledge of what procedures to use, when to use them, and how to use them (National Research Council, 2001). Notice that procedural fluency is more than just memorizing and executing procedures, algorithms, and steps. Again, procedural fluency is relational understanding of procedures, algorithms, and steps.

Before moving forward, take a moment and connect conceptual knowledge to procedural fluency. How are these ideas connected?

_____

_____

_____

_____

The "what" of procedural fluency is dependent on conceptual knowledge. Conceptual knowledge helps us understand the when and how of procedures, algorithms, and steps.

When procedural fluency is an essential part of our mathematics teaching and learning, our students understand the rules and the reasons. Whether calculating the area of a polygon, determining the slope of a line, or finding the area under the curve, learners demonstrate their procedural fluency when they can utilize specific procedures, algorithms, and steps with flexibility, accuracy, and efficiency.

Drawing from your experiences in teaching and learning mathematics, summarize what you believe is meant by the following three features of procedural fluency:

Flexibility:

_____

_____

Accuracy:

_____

_____

Efficiency:

_____

_____

Learners must use procedures, algorithms, and steps flexibly in a mathematics problem. For example, if the coefficient in front of the square term is negative, learners may have to multiply both sides by "–1" before solving the quadratic. Learners must also be accurate in their approach to solving a mathematics problem. Using a specific algorithm to find the set of all numbers that are a solution to a linear inequality still requires that they accurately divide both sides by a "–2" and be accurate in that computation. Finally, learners must know how to use a procedure efficiently so that they do not consume too much working memory. For example, if the sides of a triangle represent a Pythagorean triplet, learners should recognize this and use their conceptual knowledge to more efficiently determine congruency.

> Before moving to strategic competence, let's take time to flip back to the statement chart from the Georgia Department of Education (2021) on p. 19. Using a third color of highlighter or writing utensil from the previous tasks, identify the procedural fluency that students must have to demonstrate proficiency in this specific standard. To get you started, we would highlight the term *solve*.

Again, hang on to your responses. We will bring these together very soon.

*Strategic Competence.* Conceptual knowledge and procedural fluency, alone, do not reflect mathematics proficiency. For example, consider the concepts of area and perimeter. At their core, these concepts are associated with procedural fluency in calculating the area and perimeter of a given shape. However, mathematics proficiency must include the capacity of the learner to recognize when these two concepts and their associated procedures are applicable to a given context. Consider the two problems below and see if you can recognize which one requires strategic competence:

- **Problem #1:** Find the area of a rectangle with a length of 15 cm and a width of 6 cm. What is the perimeter of this rectangle?

- **Problem #2:** The school soccer field is 65 yards by 35 yards. If the players dribble the ball around the field four times in practice, how many total yards did they dribble the soccer ball during practice?

> How are these problems similar? How are they different? Which problem requires strategic competence? Use the space provided to describe what you think is meant by strategic competence.
>
> _____
>
> _____
>
> _____
>
> _____

Problem #2 requires learners to first represent the problem using numbers, symbols, or models/visual representations. From there, learners must identify the relationships within the problem to develop an approach for solving the problem. The capacity for learners to identify these relationships moves them away from simply grabbing numbers and plugging them into a formula. Instead, learners are more flexible and efficient in utilizing specific procedures to arrive at a mathematically accurate solution.

Strategic competence pulls together conceptual knowledge and procedural fluency. Strategic competence relies on relational understanding of the mathematics. Proficiency here is demonstrated by learners' ability to formulate, represent, and solve mathematics problems (National Research Council, 2001).

Take a moment and review your responses to the previous tasks around the sixth-grade Georgia standard. At this point, you have identified where relational understanding is called out in the standard, as well as the conceptual knowledge and procedural fluency expected in this chunk of mathematics learning.

In the space provided, analyze those three previous responses on pages 20, 22, and 23. Describe the level of strategic competence present within this standard. For example, where are learners expected to represent a mathematical problem, identify specific relationships, and then develop an approach for solving the problem? Write these specific examples here.

_____

_____

_____

_____

*Adaptive Reasoning.* This element of mathematics learning—a part of what it means to be proficient in mathematics—zeros in on the thinking of learners. Let's pull two problems from the beginning of this module to highlight this specific element of mathematics learning.

1. Subtract: $\frac{9}{10} - \frac{2}{5}$. Write your answer in simplest form.

   Describe the steps you took to find the solution to this problem.

   _____

   _____

2. The migration pattern of a species of birds to different areas over the course of a year can be represented using the graph below. Create a table of *x-values* and *y-values* and express whether the pattern follows a linear function.

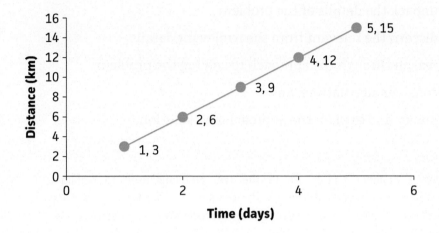

| X | Y |
|---|---|
|   |   |

If the migratory pattern is linear, express how the constant change in y corresponds to a constant change in x.

_____

_____

Both problems require adaptive reasoning. Learners must not only have the conceptual knowledge and procedural fluency to demonstrate strategic competence, but learners must think logically to perform the following (Battista, 2017; Darwani et al., 2020; Muin et al., 2018):

1. unpack the details of the problem,

2. discern the relevant from the irrelevant details,

3. reason through the approach to solving the problem,

4. consider alternatives, and

5. justify and explain the approach and solution.

---

Take a moment and return to the two problems used to highlight adaptive reasoning. Walk through the components of adaptive reasoning with each problem. Jot down your thoughts, challenges, and questions here.

_____

_____

_____

_____

---

*Productive Dispositions.* The final element of mathematics learning brings us face to face with learners' general disposition toward mathematics. Do learners find mathematics relevant? Do learners see value in mathematics? Finally, what are learners' attitudes toward mathematics and toward themselves as mathematics learners? Yes, we are talking about attitudes, beliefs, engagement, and efficacy. Productive dispositions develop alongside the other elements of mathematics learning, and we can be intentional, purposeful, and deliberate in developing these dispositions. For example, we can focus on the disposition of persistence in problem solving during a particular unit. Maybe we focus on the usefulness of mathematics during a unit that integrates science. The access and opportunity to engage in the highest level of learning possible enhances the productive dispositions of learners in mathematics. Our conversation regarding productive dispositions is a perfect segue into our next module.

Learners' attitudes, beliefs, engagement, and efficacy are integral parts of their mathematics learning journey. Furthermore, this is where we play a major role in that journey.

As we transition out of this module and into Module #2, take a moment and reflect on the value of productive dispositions on mathematics learning. What happens if learners do not have the access and opportunity to develop conceptual knowledge? Procedural fluency? Strategic competence? Adaptive reasoning? As mathematics teachers, lead teachers, coaches, and instructional leaders, we must first recognize and understand the elements to mathematics learning. But we cannot stop there if we are to implement what works best in mathematics teaching and learning. We must take this information and translate these ideas into approaches, strategies, and interventions that foster, nurture, and sustain each of these elements. This development of mathematics proficiency amplifies learners' progress toward relational understanding—rules and reason. Given that the most influential factor on a student's learning journey, for which we have control, is the teacher (Rickards et al., 2021), that is where we will devote our attention from this point forward in this Playbook. How do we, not by chance but by design, foster, nurture, and sustain these elements in our mathematics teaching?

Let's return to the table on pages 14–15 in this module. You were asked to analyze several problems and identify what learners would need to know, understand, and be able to do to successfully solve those problems. You likely filled up the right column with various content, skills, and understandings. Take a moment and return to that table and mark your responses in the right column based on the element of mathematics learning represented in your responses. Use the following key to complete the task:

- Put a **C** next to those responses that represent conceptual knowledge.

- Put a **P** next to those responses that represent procedural fluency.

- Put an **S** next to those responses that represent strategic competence.

- Put an **A** next to those responses that represent adaptive reasoning.

- Put a **D** next to those responses that represent productive dispositions.

# Exit Ticket

Take a moment and self-evaluate your own learning in this module using these statements.

1. I can compare and contrast the two different types of mathematics understanding.

| 1 | 2 | 3 | 4 | 5 |
|---|---|---|---|---|
| Strongly disagree | Disagree | Neutral | Agree | Strongly agree |

Explain the reason for your selection.

_____

_____

2. I can identify the different elements of mathematics learning.

| 1 | 2 | 3 | 4 | 5 |
|---|---|---|---|---|
| Strongly disagree | Disagree | Neutral | Agree | Strongly agree |

Explain the reason for your selection.

_____

_____

3. I can recognize these elements in standards and curriculum documents.

| 1 | 2 | 3 | 4 | 5 |
|---|---|---|---|---|
| Strongly disagree | Disagree | Neutral | Agree | Strongly agree |

Explain the reason for your selection.

_____

_____

# How Do I Identify the Elements of Mathematics Teaching and Learning for My Classroom?

## MODULE #2

**Learning Intention**

We are learning about the process for identifying the elements of mathematics teaching and learning so that we can better integrate these elements into our schools or classrooms.

**Success Criteria**

We'll know we've learned this when we can:

1.  describe the interrelated aspects that inform our mathematics teaching and learning,

2.  explain the process of analyzing a mathematics standard,

3.  use the analyzing process to identify the elements of mathematics teaching and learning in our classrooms; and

4.  describe the value added by analyzing a mathematics standard.

Describing what it means to learn mathematics or the components of mathematics teaching and learning is one thing. Identifying them in our own teaching and learning requires us to move past the general use of the terms associated with understanding and the components of understanding and to speak specifically to the local context of our classroom. Remember, our big idea from Module #1 will carry us through this module as well. Take a moment and flip back to p. 4 and rewrite **Big Idea #1** in the box below.

---

## BIG IDEA #1

Our mathematics teaching must . . . _____

_____.

---

Also, to make sure we are ready to turn our attention to our own schools and classrooms, make sure you are clear on the terminology introduced in the previous module. If you would like to record your thinking, we have provided "workspace" in Table 2.1 for you and your colleagues to review the concepts from Module #1.

**TABLE 2.1** ● Review of terminology associated with mathematics teaching and learning.

| CONCEPT | SUMMARY, DESCRIPTION, OR DEFINITION | EXAMPLE |
|---|---|---|
| Instrumental Understanding | | |
| Relational Understanding | | |
| Conceptual Knowledge | | |
| Procedural Fluency | | |
| Strategic Competence | | |
| Adaptive Reasoning | | |
| Productive Dispositions | | |

As we move forward, we need to tackle an additional idea that was introduced at the start of this module: the local context of our classroom. The local context is the multiple interrelated aspects of our specific learning environment. For example, the elements of mathematics teaching and learning may be present in our classrooms, but how they are integrated, what that integration looks like, and the specific balance between the elements depends on the unique aspects of our four learning environments. Yes, although universal themes exist across schools and mathematics classrooms, the specific nature of how we integrate the elements into our individual schools and classrooms can, should, and will be different. Take a moment and consider the interrelated aspects of your specific learning environment. What makes your classroom different from your colleagues' classrooms? What makes your classroom different from our classrooms? Use the space below to jot down some ideas. Take some time with this task—avoid deficit thinking.

Deficit thinking, as it relates to mathematics teaching and learning, is considering the individual characteristics of our students from the perspective of "lacking" some attribute, skill, or capacity. For example, thinking that learners can't read so they can't solve word problems. Another example might be the belief that learners who do not know simple multiplication facts aren't capable of solving more complex problems. Or we might believe that the parents/guardians don't have the time, skills, or interest in helping their children, and thus, the children will not learn as well as their peers. These are just a few examples of deficit thinking. We will return to this later in the Playbook. For now, let's return to the task at hand.

What makes your classroom different from your colleagues' classrooms?
What makes your classroom different from our classrooms?

_____

_____

_____

_____

To identify the elements of mathematics teaching in our own classrooms, we must consider the following interrelated aspects:

1. Standards or expectations of learning

2. Definition of mathematics learning

3. Ideal type of engagement

4. Level of readiness to learn for each of our students

5. Mathematics learning experience

6. Nature of the evidence for learning

You will see that these interrelated aspects align with the organization of this Playbook with the standards and expectations of learning at the center.

> The interrelated aspects of our classroom (Figure 2.1) can be viewed as concentric circles with each subsequent aspect enveloping the previous aspect or aspects. Take a moment and add the above aspects to the concentric circles. We got them started for you with "standards and expectations of learning."

**FIGURE 2.1** ● Interrelated aspects of our classrooms.

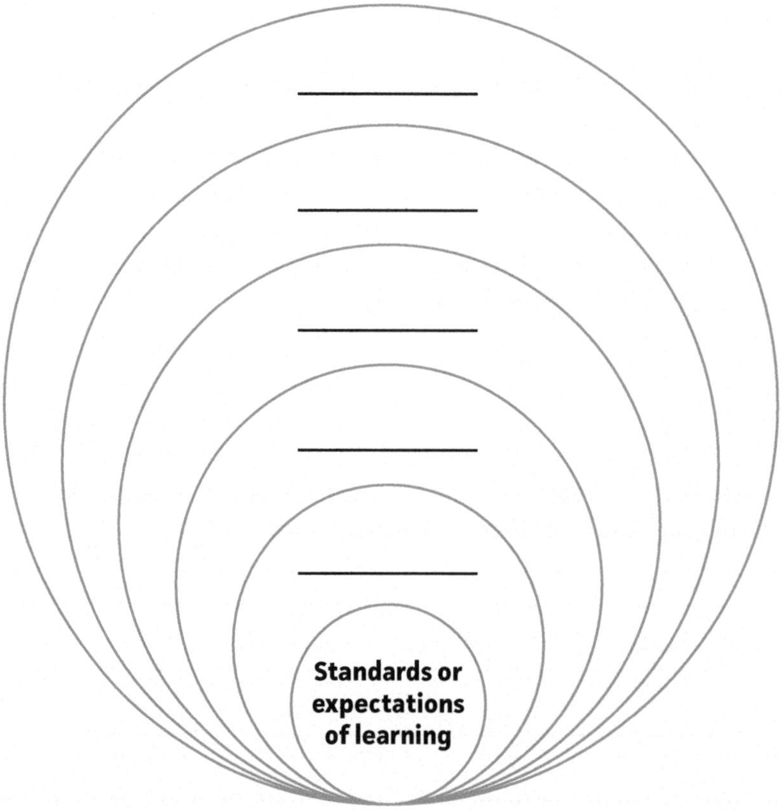

Standards or expectations of learning

To be clear, standards and expectations are not the be-all and end-all of mathematics teaching and learning. Instead, the standards and expectations articulated by our state or commonwealth lay out the specific content, skills, and understandings expected at each grade level. Analyzing these standards identifies what elements need to be addressed in a kindergarten or a calculus classroom. This is the starting point—the first play of this Playbook is to analyze specific standards and expectations. What does success look like for your grade level or in your specific level of mathematics?

In addition to using specific state standards as examples, we will continue to provide other examples on the companion website for this Playbook (e.g., Common Core State Standards, California). Furthermore, we invite you to submit examples as well.

# IDENTIFYING THE ELEMENTS BY ANALYZING STANDARDS

For the next several sections of this module, you will be very busy identifying the elements of mathematics teaching and learning in your own classroom. To get ready for these next several tasks, take a moment and gather the mathematics standards for your school, district, or state. In addition, grab any curriculum documents provided to you or created by you to support the standards. We will let you know when to use them, but for now, just have them ready to go.

We will try to strike a delicate balance over the next several sections of this module. We recognize that analyzing standards is often viewed as a thing of the past—been there, done that. At the same time, the mathematics standards articulate the expectations regarding understanding (instrumental versus relational), conceptual knowledge, procedural fluency, strategic competence, adaptive reasoning, and productive dispositions for a specific grade-level or mathematics course. Furthermore, as standards are revised or changed to reflect new research on mathematics teaching and learning, we must revise our approaches in the classroom. Furthermore, our thinking about the expectations articulated in the standards changes over the years as we implement lessons designed to build students' competency with the content. So, let's get started. The process of analyzing standards involves the following:

1. Underlining the concepts, key vocabulary, and ideas contained within a specific standard. This part of the process helps us grasp the "what" of mathematics learning. What are students learning in this standard?

2. Then, we circle the verbs linked to those concepts, key vocabulary, and ideas. The verbs communicate how well our students are expected to know those concepts, key vocabulary, and ideas. This process is often identified as the level of rigor in a particular standard.

3. The standard is then reviewed one final time to extract processes and practices, or the ways of working and thinking, of mathematicians. Simply square or box in those processes and practices.

That is an overview of the process.

After reading through the analyzing process, take a moment and compare these steps with what you already do with your grade-level, content-area, or professional learning community (PLC+) team. What do you already do and do well? Where might you see opportunities for growth? Use the space below to jot down the thoughts of you and your colleagues.

_____

_____

_____

_____

Now let's walk through the process using a model we created for you, followed by an opportunity for you and your colleagues to engage in guided practice, and then share a template for you to do this on your own at your next grade-level, content-area, or PLC+ meeting.

## A MODEL FOR ANALYZING STANDARDS

**Georgia Mathematics Standard G.GSR.7.2**

bit.ly/3NMWvfa

We will model this process using specific standards that we have selected as models for this work. Consider the Geometric and Spatial Reasoning—Trigonometry and the Unit Circle Standard, part of the *Georgia K–12 Mathematics Standards* from the Georgia Department of Education (2021). For the full standard and all supporting documents, please use the QR code in the margin to access these documents. We will walk through this process using parts of this standard with the understanding that you would apply this process to each component of the standard. For example, each mathematics standard in Georgia includes the following:

1. Expecations

2. Evidence of Student Learning

3. Strategies and Methods

4. Fundamentals

For each step of the analyzing process, you would apply the particular work to all four of those components. For space purposes, we will only provide an example of specific components.

Let's go through the process presented on the previous page to see how this would look with this standard.

1. Underlining the concepts, key vocabulary, and ideas contained within a specific standard.

| G.GSR.7.2 | Explore and explain the <u>relationship</u> between radian measures and <u>degree measures</u> and convert fluently between <u>degree</u> and <u>radian</u> measures. | **Fundamentals**<br><br>• Students should be able to convert fluently (flexibly, accurately, and efficiently) between <u>degree</u> and <u>radian</u> <u>measures</u> to solve real-life problems. | **Strategies and Methods**<br><br>• Students should have opportunities to explore and discover experimentally the <u>relationship</u> between <u>radian</u> <u>measure</u> and <u>degree measure</u> using <u>visual tools.</u> |
|---|---|---|---|

Source: Georgia Department of Education, 2021.

Again, we only modeled this process for one row of the standard.

2. Circle the verbs linked to those concepts, key vocabulary, and ideas.

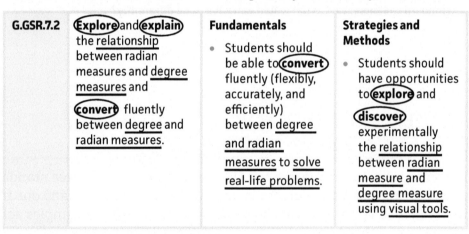

| G.GSR.7.2 | (Explore) and (explain) the <u>relationship</u> between radian measures and <u>degree measures</u> and (convert) fluently between <u>degree</u> and <u>radian measures.</u> | **Fundamentals**<br><br>• Students should be able to (convert) fluently (flexibly, accurately, and efficiently) between <u>degree</u> and <u>radian</u> <u>measures</u> to <u>solve</u> real-life problems. | **Strategies and Methods**<br><br>• Students should have opportunities to (explore) and (discover) experimentally the <u>relationship</u> between <u>radian</u> <u>measure</u> and <u>degree measure</u> using <u>visual tools.</u> |
|---|---|---|---|

Source: Georgia Department of Education, 2021.

3. Reviewed the standard one final time to box in processes and practices, or the ways of working and thinking of mathematicians.

| G.GSR.7.2 | Explore and [explain] [the relationship] between radian measures and degree measures and convert fluently between degree and radian measures. | Fundamentals | Strategies and Methods |
|---|---|---|---|
| | | • Students should be able to convert fluently (flexibly, accurately, and efficiently) between degree and radian measures to solve real-life problems. | • Students should have opportunities to explore and discover experimentally the relationwship between radian measure and degree measure using visual tools. |

**Source:** Georgia Department of Education, 2021.

Take a moment and talk through the previous process. If possible, talk through the process with colleagues. Would you have approached this standard the same way? What would you have done differently?

**Indiana Mathematics Standard 3.AT**
bit.ly/47HXZPt

**Indiana Mathematics Standard 7.AT**
bit.ly/4698bPD

**Indiana Mathematics Standard AI.L**
bit.ly/3sptLBA

## GUIDED PRACTICE FOR ANALYZING STANDARDS

It is your turn. In the margin are URLs and QR codes for three standards from Indiana: one from elementary, one from middle grades, and one from high school algebra. We want to provide a wide range of examples across different grade levels and mathematics courses. However, the process is the same regardless of what level of mathematics we teach.

Notice that we have selected the three standards within the same strand: algebraic thinking. For the guided practice, you and your colleagues can pick one that most closely aligns with your level of mathematics or try them all!

Using the process on p. 33 and modeled previously, analyze the standard. When you are finished, we have provided suggested answers. Keep in mind that our approaches may differ based on the interrelated aspects we discussed on p. 32. Again, we will discuss that more later.

# SUGGESTED ANSWERS TO ANALYZING STANDARDS

## INDIANA'S GRADE 3 ANALYZED STANDARD EXAMPLE

1. Underlining the concepts, key vocabulary, and ideas contained within a specific standard.

| | ALGEBRAIC THINKING |
|---|---|
| **3.AT.1** | Solve real-world problems involving addition and subtraction of whole numbers within 1000 (e.g., by using drawings and equations with a symbol for the unknown number to represent the problem). |
| **3.AT.2** | Solve real-world problems involving whole number multiplication and division within 100 in situations involving equal groups, arrays, and measurement quantities (e.g., by using drawings and equations with a symbol for the unknown number to represent the problem). |
| **3.AT.3** | Solve two-step real-world problems using the four operations of addition, subtraction, multiplication and division (e.g., by using drawings and equations with a symbol for the unknown number to represent the problem). |
| **3.AT.4** | Interpret a multiplication equation as equal groups (e.g., interpret 5 × 7 as the total number of objects in 5 groups of 7 objects each). Represent verbal statements of equal groups as multiplication equations. |
| **3.AT.5** | Determine the unknown whole number in a multiplication or division equation relating three whole numbers. |
| **3.AT.6** | Create, extend, and give an appropriate rule for number patterns within 100 (including patterns in the addition table or multiplication table). |

**Source:** Excerpt of the Indiana Department of Education State Standards (2020).

2. Circle the verbs linked to those concepts, key vocabulary, and ideas.

| | ALGEBRAIC THINKING |
|---|---|
| **3.AT.1** | Solve real-world problems involving addition and subtraction of whole numbers within 1000 (e.g., by using drawings and equations with a symbol for the unknown number to represent the problem). |
| **3.AT.2** | Solve real-world problems involving whole number multiplication and division within 100 in situations involving equal groups, arrays, and measurement quantities (e.g., by using drawings and equations with a symbol for the unknown number to represent the problem). |
| **3.AT.3** | Solve two-step real-world problems using the four operations of addition, subtraction, multiplication and division (e.g., by using drawings and equations with a symbol for the unknown number to represent the problem). |
| **3.AT.4** | Interpret a multiplication equation as equal groups (e.g., interpret 5 × 7 as the total number of objects in 5 groups of 7 objects each). Represent verbal statements of equal groups as multiplication equations. |
| **3.AT.5** | Determine the unknown whole number in a multiplication or division equation relating three whole numbers. |
| **3.AT.6** | Create, extend, and give an appropriate rule for number patterns within 100 (including patterns in the addition table or multiplication table). |

**Source:** Excerpt of the Indiana Department of Education State Standards (2020).

3. Reviewed the standard one final time to box in processes and practices, or the ways of working and thinking of mathematicians.

### ALGEBRAIC THINKING

| | |
|---|---|
| **3.AT.1** | Solve real-world problems involving addition and subtraction of whole numbers within 1000 (e.g., by using drawings and equations with a symbol for the unknown number to represent the problem). |
| **3.AT.2** | Solve real-world problems involving whole number multiplication and division within 100 in situations involving equal groups, arrays, and measurement quantities (e.g., by using drawings and equations with a symbol for the unknown number to represent the problem). |
| **3.AT.3** | Solve two-step real-world problems using the four operations of addition, subtraction, multiplication and division (e.g., by using drawings and equations with a symbol for the unknown number to represent the problem). |
| **3.AT.4** | Interpret a multiplication equation as equal groups (e.g., interpret 5 × 7 as the total number of objects in 5 groups of 7 objects each). Represent verbal statements of equal groups as multiplication equations. |
| **3.AT.5** | Determine the unknown whole number in a multiplication or division equation relating three whole numbers. |
| **3.AT.6** | Create, extend, and give an appropriate rule for number patterns within 100 (including patterns in the addition table or multiplication table). |

**Source:** Excerpt of the Indiana Department of Education State Standards (2020).

## INDIANA'S GRADE 7 ANALYZED STANDARD EXAMPLE

1. Underlining the concepts, key vocabulary, and ideas contained within a specific standard.

### ALGEBRA AND FUNCTIONS

| | |
|---|---|
| **7.AF.1** | Apply the properties of operations (e.g., identity, inverse, commutative, associative, distributive properties) to create equivalent linear expressions, including situations that involve factoring out a common number (e.g., given $2x - 10$, create an equivalent expression $2(x - 5)$). Justify each step in the process. |
| **7.AF.2** | Solve equations of the form $px + q = r$ and $p(x + q) = r$ fluently, where p, q, and r are specific rational numbers. Represent real-world problems using equations of these forms and solve such problems. |
| **7.AF.3** | Solve inequalities of the form $px + q$ (> or ≥) r or $px + q$ (< or ≤) r, where p, q, and r are specific rational numbers. Represent real-world problems using inequalities of these forms and solve such problems. Graph the solution set of the inequality and interpret it in the context of the problem. |
| **7.AF.4** | Define slope as vertical change for each unit of horizontal change and recognize that a constant rate of change or constant slope describes a linear function. Identify and describe situations with constant or varying rates of change. |
| **7.AF.5** | Graph a line given its slope and a point on the line. Find the slope of a line given its graph. |
| **7.AF.6** | Decide whether two quantities are in a proportional relationship (e.g., by testing for equivalent ratios in a table or graphing on a coordinate plane and observing whether the graph is a straight line through the origin). |
| **7.AF.7** | Identify the unit rate or constant of proportionality in tables, graphs, equations, and verbal descriptions of proportional relationships. |
| **7.AF.8** | Explain what the coordinates of a point on the graph of a proportional relationship mean in terms of the situation, with special attention to the points (0, 0) and (1,r), where r is the unit rate. |
| **7.AF.9** | Represent real-world and other mathematical situations that involve proportional relationships. Write equations and draw graphs to represent these proportional relationships. Recognize that these situations are described by a linear function in the form y = mx, where the unit rate, m, is the slope of the line. |

**Source:** Excerpt of the Indiana Department of Education State Standards (2020).

2. Circle the verbs linked to those concepts, key vocabulary, and ideas.

| ALGEBRA AND FUNCTIONS | |
|---|---|
| **7.AF.1** | (Apply) the properties of operations (e.g., identity, inverse, commutative, associative, distributive properties) to (create) equivalent linear expressions, including situations that involve factoring out a common number (e.g., given 2x – 10, create an equivalent expression 2(x – 5)). (Justify) each step in the process. |
| **7.AF.2** | (Solve) equations of the form px + q = r and p(x + q) = r fluently, where p, q, and r are specific rational numbers. (Represent) real-world problems using equations of these forms and solve such problems. |
| **7.AF.3** | (Solve) inequalities of the form px + q (> or ≥) r or px + q (< or ≤) r, where p, q, and r are specific rational numbers. (Represent) real-world problems using inequalities of these forms and solve such problems. (Graph) the solution set of the inequality and interpret it in the context of the problem. |
| **7.AF.4** | (Define) slope as vertical change for each unit of horizontal change and recognize that a constant rate of change or constant slope describes a linear function. (Identify) and (describe) situations with constant or varying rates of change. |
| **7.AF.5** | (Graph) a line given its slope and a point on the line. (Find) the slope of a line given its graph. |
| **7.AF.6** | (Decide) whether two quantities are in a proportional relationship (e.g., by testing for equivalent ratios in a table or graphing on a coordinate plane and observing whether the graph is a straight line through the origin). |
| **7.AF.7** | (Identify) the unit rate or constant of proportionality in tables, graphs, equations, and verbal descriptions of proportional relationships. |
| **7.AF.8** | (Explain) what the coordinates of a point on the graph of a proportional relationship mean in terms of the situation, with special attention to the points (0, 0) and (1,r), where r is the unit rate. |
| **7.AF.9** | (Represent) real-world and other mathematical situations that involve proportional relationships. (Write) equations and draw graphs to represent these proportional relationships. (Recognize) that these situations are described by a linear function in the form y = mx, where the unit rate, m, is the slope of the line. |

**Source:** Excerpt of the Indiana Department of Education State Standards (2020).

3. Reviewed the standard one final time to box in processes and practices, or the ways of working and thinking of mathematicians.

| ALGEBRA AND FUNCTIONS | |
|---|---|
| **7.AF.1** | Apply the properties of operations (e.g., identity, inverse, commutative, associative, distributive properties) to create equivalent linear expressions, including situations that involve factoring out a common number (e.g., given 2x – 10, create an equivalent expression 2(x – 5)). Justify each step in the process. |
| **7.AF.2** | Solve equations of the form px + q = r and p(x + q) = r fluently, where p, q, and r are specific rational numbers. Represent real-world problems using equations of these forms and solve such problems. |
| **7.AF.3** | Solve inequalities of the form px +q (> or ≥) r or px + q (< or ≤) r, where p, q, and r are specific rational numbers. Represent real-world problems using inequalities of these forms and solve such problems. Graph the solution set of the inequality and interpret it in the context of the problem. |
| **7.AF.4** | Define slope as vertical change for each unit of horizontal change and recognize that a constant rate of change or constant slope describes a linear function. Identify and describe situations with constant or varying rates of change. |
| **7.AF.5** | Graph a line given its slope and a point on the line. Find the slope of a line given its graph. |
| **7.AF.6** | Decide whether two quantities are in a proportional relationship (e.g., by testing for equivalent ratios in a table or graphing on a coordinate plane and observing whether the graph is a straight line through the origin). |
| **7.AF.7** | Identify the unit rate or constant of proportionality in tables, graphs, equations, and verbal descriptions of proportional relationships. |
| **7.AF.8** | Explain what the coordinates of a point on the graph of a proportional relationship mean in terms of the situation, with special attention to the points (0, 0) and (1,r), where r is the unit rate. |
| **7.AF.9** | Represent real-world and other mathematical situations that involve proportional relationships. Write equations and draw graphs to represent these proportional relationships. Recognize that these situations are described by a linear function in the form y = mx, where the unit rate, m, is the slope of the line. |

**Source:** Excerpt of the Indiana Department of Education State Standards (2020).

# INDIANA'S ALGEBRA ANALYZED
# STANDARD EXAMPLE

1. Underlining the concepts, key vocabulary, and ideas contained within a specific standard.

| | LINEAR EQUATIONS, INEQUALITIES, AND FUNCTIONS |
|---|---|
| **AI.L.1** | Represent real-world problems using linear equations and inequalities in one variable, including those with rational number coefficients and variables on both sides of the equal sign. Solve them fluently, explaining the process used and justifying the choice of a solution method. |
| **AI.L.2** | Solve compound linear inequalities in one variable, and represent and solution on a number line. Write a compound linear interpret the inequality given its number line representation. |
| **AI.L.3** | Represent linear functions as graphs from equations (with and without technology), equations from graphs, and equations from tables and other given information(e.g., from a given point on a line and the slope of the line). Find the equation of a line, passing through a given point, that is parallel or perpendicular to a given line. |
| **AI.L.4** | Represent real-world problems that can be modeled with a linear function using equations, graphs, and tables; translate fluently among these representations, and interpret the slope and intercepts. |
| **AI.L.5** | Translate among equivalent forms of equations for linear functions, including slope-intercept, point-slope, and standard. Recognize that different forms reveal more or less information about a given situation. |
| **AI.L.6** | Represent real-world problems using linear inequalities in two variables and solve such problems; interpret the solution set and determine whether it is reasonable. Graph the solutions to a linear inequality in two variables as a half-plane. |
| **AI.L.7** | Solve linear and quadratic equations and formulas for a specified variable to highlight a quantity of interest, using the same reasoning as in solving equations. |

**Source:** Excerpt of the Indiana Department of Education State Standards (2020).

2. Circle the verbs linked to those concepts, key vocabulary, and ideas.

| | LINEAR EQUATIONS, INEQUALITIES, AND FUNCTIONS |
|---|---|
| **AI.L.1** | Represent real-world problems using linear equations and inequalities in one variable, including those with rational number coefficients and variables on both sides of the equal sign. Solve them fluently, explaining the process used and justifying the choice of a solution method. |
| **AI.L.2** | Solve compound linear inequalities in one variable, and represent and interpret the solution on a number line. Write a compound linear inequality given its number line representation. |
| **AI.L.3** | Represent linear functions as graphs from equations (with and without technology), equations from graphs, and equations from tables and other given information (e.g., from a given point on a line and the slope of the line). Find the equation of a line, passing through a given point, that is parallel or perpendicular to a given line. |
| **AI.L.4** | Represent real-world problems that can be modeled with a linear function using equations, graphs, and tables; translate fluently among these representations, and interpret the slope and intercepts. |
| **AI.L.5** | Translate among equivalent forms of equations for linear functions, including slope-intercept, point-slope, and standard. Recognize that different forms reveal more or less information about a given situation. |
| **AI.L.6** | Represent real-world problems using linear inequalities in two variables and solve such problems; interpret the solution set and determine whether it is reasonable. Graph the solutions to a linear inequality in two variables as a half-plane. |
| **AI.L.7** | Solve linear and quadratic equations and formulas for a specified variable to highlight a quantity of interest, using the same reasoning as in solving equations. |

**Source:** Excerpt of the Indiana Department of Education State Standards (2020).

3. Reviewed the standard one final time to box in processes and practices, or the ways of working and thinking of mathematicians.

| | LINEAR EQUATIONS, INEQUALITIES, AND FUNCTIONS |
|---|---|
| **AI.L.1** | Represent real-world problems using linear equations and inequalities in one variable, including those with rational number coefficients and variables on both sides of the equal sign. Solve them fluently, explaining the process used and justifying the choice of a solution method. |
| **AI.L.2** | Solve compound linear inequalities in one variable, and represent and solution on a number line. Write a compound linear interpret the inequality given its number line representation. |
| **AI.L.3** | Represent linear functions as graphs from equations (with and without technology), equations from graphs, and equations from tables and other given information(e.g., from a given point on a line and the slope of the line). Find the equation of a line, passing through a given point, that is parallel or perpendicular to a given line. |
| **AI.L.4** | Represent real-world problems that can be modeled with a linear function using equations, graphs, and tables; translate fluently among these representations, and interpret the slope and intercepts. |
| **AI.L.5** | Translate among equivalent forms of equations for linear functions, including slope-intercept, point-slope, and standard. Recognize that different forms reveal more or less information about a given situation. |
| **AI.L.6** | Represent real-world problems using linear inequalities in two variables and solve such problems; interpret the solution set and determine whether it is reasonable. Graph the solutions to a linear inequality in two variables as a half-plane. |
| **AI.L.7** | Solve linear and quadratic equations and formulas for a specified variable to highlight a quantity of interest, using the same reasoning as in solving equations. |

**Source:** Excerpt of the Indiana Department of Education State Standards (2020).

## PUTTING THE PLAYBOOK TO USE IN YOUR MATHEMATICS TEACHING

Do you remember when we asked you to gather the mathematics standards for your school, district, or state, along with any curriculum documents provided to you or created by you to support the standards? Well, now we are going to put those into action. Our hope is that you have pulled a standard that is the focus of an upcoming unit. This Playbook is most effective when the tasks and experiences in these modules are immediately applicable to our schools and classrooms.

On the actual standard and curriculum documents, underline the concepts, key vocabulary, and terms. Circle the verbs. Box in the processes and practices (Figures 2.2 and 2.3). Then, use the space provided to record the result of that analysis (Figures 2.4 and 2.5). We have provided an example from the model using the Georgia Standards on p. 35.

**FIGURE 2.2** ● Third grade analyzing the standard comprehensive document.

| GRADE LEVEL/CONTENT AREA: *THIRD-GRADE MATHEMATICS* STANDARD(S): *3.AT* | STRAND: *ALGEBRAIC THINKING* |
|---|---|
| **Underlined concepts, key vocabulary, and ideas:** | **Circled verbs (line them up with the concepts, key vocabulary, and ideas to which they are linked):** |
| *Real-world problems (multiple mentions)* | *Solve* |
| *Addition* | |
| *Subtraction* | |
| *Whole numbers within 1,000 (multiple mentions)* | |
| *Drawings* | |
| *Equations with a symbol* | |
| *Unknown number* | |
| *Multiplication* | |
| *Division* | *Solve* |
| *Whole number* | |
| *Equal groups* | |
| *Arrays* | |
| *Measurement quantities* | |
| *Two-step real-world problems* | *Solve* |
| *Operations* | |
| *Multiplication equations* | *Interpret* |
| *Equal groups* | |
| *Verbal statements* | |
| *Unknown whole number* | *Determine* |
| *Division equation* | |
| *Relating* | |
| *Appropriate rule* | *Create* |
| *Number patterns within 100* | *Extend* |
| *Patterns* | *Give* |
| *Addition Table* | |
| *Multiplication Table* | |

**Processes and Practices:**

*Real-world problem solving*

*Using drawing and equations with a symbol for the unknown number to represent the problem*

*Interpret*

*Patterns*

**FIGURE 2.3** ● Seventh grade analyzing the standard comprehensive document.

| GRADE LEVEL/CONTENT AREA: *SEVENTH-GRADE MATHEMATICS* STANDARD(S): *3.AF* | STRAND: *ALGEBRA AND FUNCTIONS* |
|---|---|
| **Underlined concepts, key vocabulary, and ideas:** | **Circled verbs (line them up with the concepts, key vocabulary, and ideas to which they are linked):** |
| Properties of operations | Apply |
| Identity | Create |
| Inverse | Justify |
| Commutative | |
| Associative | |
| Distributive | |
| Equivalent linear expressions | |
| Factoring out a common number | |
| Equations | Solve |
| Form $px + q = r$, $p(x + q)$ | Represent |
| Specific rational numbers | |
| Real-world problems | |
| Inequalities | Solve |
| Form $px + q <$ or $> r$, $p(x + q) <$ or $> r$ | Represent |
| Problems | Graph |
| Solution Set | |
| Context of the Problem | |
| Slope | Define |
| Vertical change | Identify |
| Unit | Describe |
| Horizontal change | |
| Constant rate of change | |
| Constant slope | |
| Linear function | |
| Constant | |
| Varying rates of change | |
| Line | Graph |
| Slope | Find |
| Point on the line | |
| Graph | |

| GRADE LEVEL/CONTENT AREA: SEVENTH-GRADE MATHEMATICS STANDARD(S): 3.AF | STRAND: ALGEBRA AND FUNCTIONS |
|---|---|
| Quantities | Decide |
| Proportional relationship | |
| Equivalent ratios | |
| Table | |
| Graphing | |
| Coordinate plane | |
| Straight line | |
| Origin | |
| Unit rate | Identify |
| Constant of proportionality | |
| Tables | |
| Verbal descriptions of proportional relationships | |
| Coordinates | Explain |
| Points on the graph | |
| Situation | |
| Points | |
| (0,0) | |
| (1, r) | |
| Unit rate | |
| Mathematical situations | Represent |
| Linear function | Write |
| Form y = mx + b | Recognize |
| M | |

**Processes and Practices:**

Justify

Real-world problem solving

Decide

Explain

**FIGURE 2.4** ● Algebra analyzing the standard comprehensive document.

| GRADE LEVEL/CONTENT AREA: ALGEBRA | STRAND: LINEAR EQUATIONS, INEQUALITIES, AND FUNCTIONS |
|---|---|
| STANDARD(S): *AI.L* | |
| **Underlined concepts, key vocabulary, and ideas:** | **Circled verbs (line them up with the concepts, key vocabulary, and ideas to which they are linked):** |
| Real-world problems | Represent |
| Linear equations | Explaining |
| Inequalities in one-variable | Justifying |
| Rational number coefficients | |
| Variables | |
| Both sides of the equal sign | |
| Process | |
| Choice of solution method | |
| Compound linear inequalities | Solve |
| One variable | Write |
| Solution | |
| Number line | |
| Compound linear inequality | |
| Number line representation | |
| Linear functions | Represent |
| Graphs from equations | Find |
| Equations | |
| Graphs | |
| Equations from tables | |
| Given point | |
| Line | |
| Slope of the line | |
| Equation of a line | |
| Passing through a given point | |
| Parallel to a given line | |
| Perpendicular to a given line | |

| GRADE LEVEL/CONTENT AREA: ALGEBRA STANDARD(S): AI.L | STRAND: LINEAR EQUATIONS, INEQUALITIES, AND FUNCTIONS |
|---|---|
| Representations | Represent |
| Slope | Translate |
| Intercepts | Interpret |
| Equivalent forms of linear functions | Translate |
| Slope-intercept | Recognize |
| Point-slope | |
| Standard | |
| Different forms | |
| Two variables | Represent |
| Such problems | Solve |
| Solution set | Interpret |
| Reasonable (regarding solution set) | Determine |
| Solutions | Graph |
| Linear inequality | |
| Half-plane | |
| Quadratic equations | Solve |
| Formulas | |
| Specified variable | |
| Quantity of interest | |
| Reasoning | |

**Processes and Practices:**

Real-world problem solving

Justify

With and without technology

Modeling

Reasoning

**FIGURE 2.5** ● Analyzing the standard comprehensive document template.

| GRADE LEVEL/CONTENT AREA: STANDARD(S): | STRAND: |
|---|---|
| Underlined concepts, key vocabulary, and ideas:<br><br>_____<br><br>_____<br><br>_____<br><br>_____ | Circled verbs (line them up with the concepts, key vocabulary, and ideas to which they are linked):<br><br>_____<br><br>_____<br><br>_____<br><br>_____ |
| **Processes and Practices:**<br><br>_____ ||

online resources ⟍ This resource is available for download at **resources.corwin.com/themathematicsplaybook**.

Make sure to mark this page. We will come back here several times throughout the Playbook.

## Exit Ticket

Take a moment and self-evaluate your learning in this module using these statements.

1. I can describe the interrelated aspects that inform our mathematics teaching and learning.

| 1 | 2 | 3 | 4 | 5 |
|---|---|---|---|---|
| Strongly disagree | Disagree | Neutral | Agree | Strongly agree |

Explain the reason for your selection.

_____

_____

2. I can explain the process of analyzing a mathematics standard.

| 1 | 2 | 3 | 4 | 5 |
|---|---|---|---|---|
| Strongly disagree | Disagree | Neutral | Agree | Strongly agree |

Explain the reason for your selection.

_____

_____

3. I can use the analyzing process to identify the elements of mathematics teaching and learning in my classroom.

| 1 | 2 | 3 | 4 | 5 |
|---|---|---|---|---|
| Strongly disagree | Disagree | Neutral | Agree | Strongly agree |

Explain the reason for your selection.

_____

_____

4. I can describe the value added by analyzing a mathematics standard.

| 1 | 2 | 3 | 4 | 5 |
|---|---|---|---|---|
| Strongly disagree | Disagree | Neutral | Agree | Strongly agree |

Explain the reason for your selection.

_____

_____

# How Do I Evaluate the Inclusion of All Aspects of Mathematics Teaching and Learning Into My Classroom?

Let's take a quick check on where we are in our learning journey. The mathematics classroom consists of a lot of moving parts. Although the beauty of mathematics is not lost on us, we do want to make sure that we are not confusing an asymptote with a hole in the graph. At this point, we have described the elements of mathematics teaching and learning. From there, we grabbed our standards and curricular documents so that we could analyze them. At the end of Module #2, we developed a list of concepts, key vocabulary, and ideas that are linked to verbs, processes, and practices. Our next step is to evaluate the inclusion of all aspects of mathematics teaching and learning into our next unit or learning experience.

# MODULE #3

How Do I Evaluate the Inclusion of All Aspects of Mathematics Teaching and Learning into

**Learning Intention**

We are developing a teaching and learning map to help us to ensure all aspects of mathematics teaching and learning are included in our classrooms.

**Success Criteria**

We'll know we've learned this when we can:

1. develop a teaching and learning map for a given standard;

2. integrate strategic competence, productive dispositions, and adaptive reasoning throughout a given standard; and

3. create a learning progression for a given standard.

To be very honest and transparent, we could easily take our standards and simply move through them like a checklist, showing learners how to solve the different types of problems and providing them with problem set after problem set in the form of worksheets, seatwork, and homework. In fact, let's take a moment to self-reflect and self-evaluate our current mathematics classroom.

Pull down a recent series of lesson plans from a previous unit or series of days. If you do not have access to these lesson plans, think back to the most recent unit or set of days in mathematics. Using the coding scheme from p. 27, complete the graph that follows showing the percentage of time you allotted for each element of mathematics teaching and learning:

- Put a **C** next to those responses that represent conceptual knowledge.

- Put a **P** next to those responses that represent procedural fluency.

- Put an **S** next to those responses that represent strategic competence.

- Put an **A** next to those responses that represent adaptive reasoning.

- Put a **D** next to those responses that represent productive dispositions.

We have provided an example of a graph for you to use as a model.

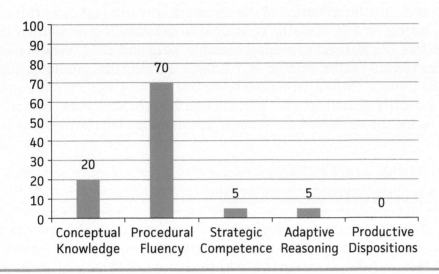

**Estimated Percentage of Time Alloted for Different Examples of Mathematics Teaching and Learning**

You will notice that this self-reflection and self-evaluation allowed the team of teachers to recognize that they emphasized procedural fluency more than any other element. Furthermore, they allotted no time for the explicit teaching and learning of productive dispositions. We will talk more about what to do next with this data. For now, we would like you and your colleagues to engage in the same self-reflection and self-evaluation of your unit or lesson plans.

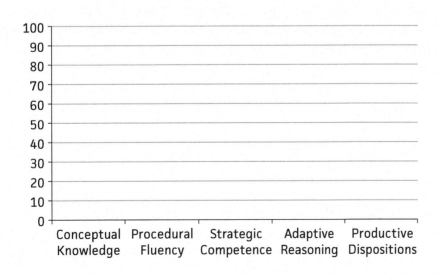

**Estimated Percentage of Time Alloted for Different Examples of Mathematics Teaching and Learning**

Your evaluation of the inclusion of all five elements may have yielded results like the example we provided. Our focus in this module is to develop ways to ensure we are incorporating all elements of mathematics learning into the tasks and experiences for our learners. As you recall from Module #1, the interrelation of the elements of mathematics learning fosters, nurtures, and sustains relational understanding of mathematics. Therefore, our learners move past a simple "plug-and-chug" view of mathematics toward usable, flexible, and durable learning that promotes mathematics literacy. Our learners then recognize identity, agency, positionality, and authority as mathematics learners (the focus of Module #4). But for now, let's tackle the estimated percentages you developed in the previous task.

## MAPPING OUT THE LEARNING PROGRESSION

One of the most effective ways to ensure we integrate all aspects into a standard, unit, or series of lessons is to take the concepts, key vocabulary, and ideas and map them out in a learning sequence. What will be the focus of Day 1, Day 2, and all the way to the final day of the standard, unit, or series of lessons. Although most standards are presented in a numbered or a bulleted list, the expectation is not, should not, and cannot be that we move through the list in that presented order. As experts in mathematics, as well as in the teaching and learning of mathematics, we have a sense of what concepts should be introduced before other ideas. We know what key vocabulary must be in place before learning about specific concepts. We are aware of what ideas learners must be comfortable with before introducing complex mathematical concepts.

Returning to the example on p. 35 and our analysis of the Trigonometry and Unit Circle standard from Georgia, we want to focus in on the list of concepts, key vocabulary, and ideas. The first step in developing a learning progression is to number the items in that left column based on the sequence of learning that we believe is best for this topic. Again, what would we introduce on Day 1, Day 2, and all the way to the final day?

| GRADE LEVEL/CONTENT AREA: *GEOMETRIC & SPATIAL REASONING*<br><br>STANDARD(S): *G.GSR.7* | STRAND:<br>*Trigonometry and the Unit Circle (Explore the concept of a radian measure and special right triangles.)* |
|---|---|
| **Underlined concepts, key vocabulary, and ideas:** | **Circled verbs (line them up with the concepts, key vocabulary, and ideas to which they are linked):** |
| Radian | Explore |
| Ratio | Interpret |
| Arc length | |
| Radius of a circle | |
| | |
| Relationship | Explore |
| Radian measures | Explain |
| Degree measures | Use |
| | Determine |
| | Identify |
| | |
| Special right triangles | Make Sense |
| Unit circle | Explore |
| Sine | Discover |
| Cosine | Using hands on tools |
| Tangent | |
| Reflections of triangles | Explore |
| Reference angles | Develop |
| Coordinate values | Convert fluently |
| Four quadrants | Articulate |
| Coordinate plane | Explore |
| Meaning of radians | Interpret |
| Visual tools | |
| Technology visualizations | Use |
| Associated radian measure | Articulate |
| Real-life problems | Develop an understanding |
| Pattern | |
| Conversions | |
| Radius units measured along the arc length of the circle | |

| GRADE LEVEL/CONTENT AREA: *GEOMETRIC & SPATIAL REASONING*<br><br>STANDARD(S): *G.GSR.7* | STRAND:<br>*Trigonometry and the Unit Circle (Explore the concept of a radian measure and special right triangles.)* | |
|---|---|---|
| **Underlined concepts, key vocabulary, and ideas:** | **Circled verbs (line them up with the concepts, key vocabulary, and ideas to which they are linked):** | |
| Radian | Explore | ① |
| Ratio | Interpret | |
| Arc length | | |
| Radius of a circle | | |
| Relationship | Explore | ③ |
| Radian measures | Explain | |
| Degree measures | Use | |
| | Determine | |
| | Identify | |
| Special right triangles | Make Sense | ④ ② |
| Unit circle | Explore | |
| Sine | Discover | |
| Cosine | Using hands on tools | |
| Tangent | | |
| Reflections of triangles | Explore | |
| Reference angles | Develop | |
| Coordinate values | Convert fluently | |
| Four quadrants | Articulate | |
| Coordinate plane | Explore | |
| Meaning of radians | Interpret | |
| Visual tools | | |
| Technology visualizations | Use | |
| Associated radian measure | Articulate | |
| Real-life problems | Develop an understanding | |
| Pattern | | |
| Conversions | | |
| Radius units measured along the arc length of the circle | | |

*(Continued)*

| | | | |
|---|---|---|---|
| Angle measures | | Angle measures | |
| Associated reflected angles | | Associated reflected angles | |
| Revolution of the unit circle | | Revolution of the unit circle | |

**Processes and Practices:**

*Interpret*

*Explain the relationship*

*Use*

*Make sense of the meaning*

*Using hands on tools*

*Real-world problem solving*

*Articulate the pattern*

*Explorations*

*Develop an understanding*

**Processes and Practices:**

*Interpret*

*Explain the relationship*

*Use*

*Make sense of the meaning*

*Using hands on tools*

*Real-world problem solving*

*Articulate the pattern*

*Explorations*

*Develop an understanding*

Notice that we propose starting the learning sequence with the parts of a circle (e.g., radius, arc length) and then transition into the idea of a radian. This process would involve the idea that a circle has a radius of 1. From there, we would move to the relationship between radians and degrees. Finally, we would then propose to introduce the four quadrants of the coordinate plane and the relationship between the unit circle and the coordinate plane.

> Your turn! Take some time and review the analysis template you and your colleagues completed at the end of Module #2. You may have completed more than one because you all decided to map out an entire year, semester, or quarter. Regardless of your choice, grab those templates and number the concepts, key vocabulary, and ideas. For now, don't worry about how many numbers you have, just number them out.

We want to make two points at this juncture in our work together. These points need to be parked in the back of our minds from now on, and we must be able to come back and revisit them often. So, please put a sticky note, a page marker, or something here so that you and your colleagues can quickly come back and find the following two points:

1. This sequence is not set in stone for the entire standard, unit, or series of lessons! Based on evidence generated during the learning tasks or experiences, we may have to adjust or change this sequence. This process is simply a proposed plan for moving into the learning and a proposed allotment of the elements of mathematics.

2. This sequence is not set in stone for next year! You may have a new class, as well as students with new strengths and opportunities to learn. A new class can equal new sets of prior experiences and background knowledge. Analzying standards is faster every year unless, of course, the standards change or you change grade levels. The sequencing of the concepts, key vocabulary, and ideas MUST be revisited, reviewed, and revised each year based on the learning needs of each new group of learners.

## LINKING THE LEARNING PROGRESSION WITH OTHER ELEMENTS

The learning sequence is now driven by concepts. That is, our sequencing of the concepts, key vocabulary, and ideas means the foundation of the teaching and learning is conceptual knowledge. Looking back at our example with Trigonometry and the Unit Circle, the concepts of arc length, radians, degrees, and the unit circle form the backbone of the tasks and learning experiences. We can think of this using a graphic organizer that visually represents this sequence.

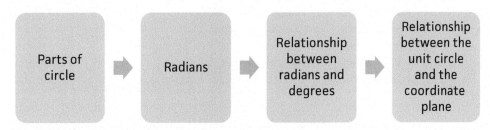

This graphic organizer simply takes the numbered concepts, key vocabulary, and ideas and arranges them into a visual representation of the standard, unit, or lesson sequence. Take a moment to do that now with your numbered analysis. However, we want you to draw the rectangles yourself because we will need to add to this graphic organizer before we conclude this module. Oh, and for those geometry teachers, yes, they are likely going to be quadrilaterals because our freehand drawings may not yield two pairs of parallel and equal-length sides.

> Using your analysis template, please create a graphic organizer of this sequence. Be sure to leave space underneath each quadrilateral for you to add additional information. We have provided examples from the Indiana standards on pp. 36–42 in Module #2.

Now the fun part begins. If this graphic organizer contains the conceptual knowledge, how do the remaining four elements fit? They are purposefully, intentionally, and deliberately integrated across the concepts. Starting with procedural fluency, this element is reflected in the circled verbs found in the standard. Which verbs are linked to which concepts? Returning to our Trigonometry and Unit Circle example, learners are expected to **explore and interpret** a radian as the ratio of the arc length to the radius of a circle. So, the part of your graphic organizer devoted to the concept of a radian would "sprout legs" to include finding the ratio of the arc length to the radius of the circle (i.e., procedural fluency). Learners must also be able to use tools in this exploration of this ratio. These are specific expectations for procedural fluency. Therefore, our graphic organizer would evolve to look like as follows:

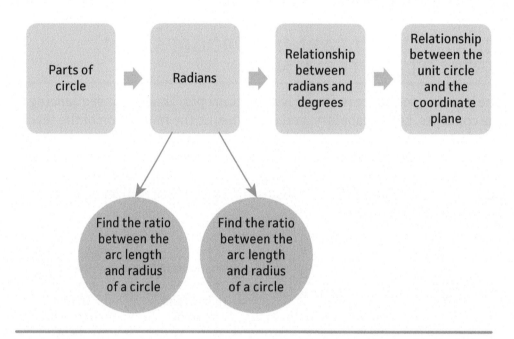

Do you see how we placed the procedural aspects of this standard with the concepts they were originally linked to in the standards document? This way, we have the right level of rigor expressed in the standard. We will dive a bit deeper into rigor in later modules, but for now, you should add the procedural fluency expectations to your graphic organizer.

Flip back to your graphic organizer on p. 57. Using your analyzing standards template, place the procedural fluency expectations in the graphic organizer.

We have provided examples from the Indiana standards on pp. 36–42 in Module #2.

# INTEGRATING STRATEGIC COMPETENCE, PRODUCTIVE DISPOSITIONS, AND ADAPTIVE REASONING

Working in the remaining elements follows the same process as the integration of procedural fluency, with one large exception. Although the verbs that point toward procedural fluency are directly linked to concepts in the standard, strategic competence, productive dispositions, and adaptive reasoning are not as obvious in their connection to concepts. However, this is great news. We have autonomy on when and where we foster, nurture, and sustain these elements. Although the processes and practices hint at possible connections, we ultimately decide how to weave in those elements that promote the identity, agency, positionality, and authority as mathematics learners.

Take a moment and review the following descriptions and definitions for strategic competence, productive dispositions, and adaptive reasoning. This will help us add these elements throughout the graphic organizer signaling where this element of mathematics teaching and learning will occur:

*Strategic Competence.* The capacity of a learner to recognize when these two concepts and their associated procedures are applicable to a given context.

*Productive Dispositions.* The learners' attitudes, beliefs, engagement, and efficacy in mathematics.

*Adaptive Reasoning.* The capacity of a learner to think logically when engaging in problem solving.

When ready to move forward, let's add these elements to our graphic organizer. Of course, we will provide examples along the way. In fact, let's start with a finished version of the Georgia Trigonometry and Unit Circle standard.

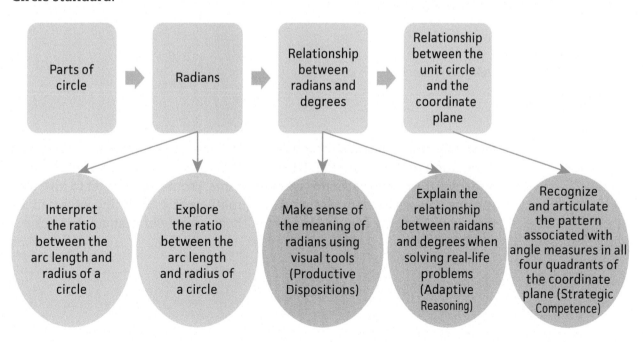

Once again, flip back to your graphic organizer on p. 57. Using your analyzing standards template, place the strategic competence, productive dispositions, and adaptive reasoning expectations in the graphic organizer.

We have provided examples from the Indiana standards on pp. 36–42 in Module #2.

## PUTTING THE PLAYBOOK TO USE IN YOUR CLASSROOM

Throughout this module, we have provided examples of graphic organizers that support the process of integrating the elements of mathematics learning into our classrooms. But the value in this Playbook comes from your integration of learning into your mathematics teaching. So, before moving to the next module, return one final time to your graphic organizer(s). Use the space below to tally up the number of opportunities in the graphic organizer for each element. Tally marks will work.

| Conceptual Knowledge |
| Procedural Fluency |
| Strategic Competence |
| Productive Dispositions |
| Adaptive Reasoning |

Now, return to your bar graph on p. 53. How do you now feel about the integration of the elements? This is as close as we can get to a before-and-after picture in our mathematics classrooms. From here, we get to dive into turning this very important work into mathematics learning experiences that move learning forward in each of these areas. But first, an exit ticket.

# Exit Ticket

Take a moment and self-evaluate your own learning in this module using these statements.

1. I can develop a teaching and learning map for a given standard.

| 1 | 2 | 3 | 4 | 5 |
|---|---|---|---|---|
| Strongly disagree | Disagree | Neutral | Agree | Strongly agree |

Explain the reason for your selection.

_____

_____

2. I can integrate strategic competence, productive dispositions, and adaptive reasoning throughout a given standard.

| 1 | 2 | 3 | 4 | 5 |
|---|---|---|---|---|
| Strongly disagree | Disagree | Neutral | Agree | Strongly agree |

Explain the reason for your selection.

_____

_____

3. We can create a learning progression for a given standard.

| 1 | 2 | 3 | 4 | 5 |
|---|---|---|---|---|
| Strongly disagree | Disagree | Neutral | Agree | Strongly agree |

Explain the reason for your selection.

_____

_____

# What Is a Mathematics Learner, and What Makes a Mathematics Learner in My Classroom?

Mathematics often evokes strong emotions—both positive or negative. Let's take a moment to identify our emotions about mathematics.

What's your reaction when you hear the word "mathematics"?

_____

_____

Draw an X along the continuum.

| I **am afraid of** math! | I'm **neutral** about math. | I **love** thinking and learning about math! |
|---|---|---|

← →

*(Continued)*

(Continued)

In Module #1, you were asked to complete eight mathematics problems. How did you feel about that task?

_____

_____

Draw an X along the continuum.

| I **struggled with the** math! | I had some success and some challenges; I was **unsure**. | I **felt successful with** math! |
|---|---|---|

We all have times where we get stuck. While you worked on the eight mathematics problems, how did you feel when you got stuck? Where would you place your reaction to those 'stuck' moments along this continuum?

_____

_____

Draw an X along the continuum.

| When I got stuck, I **gave up**! | When I got stuck, I **tried some strategies**, with some success. | When I got stuck, I told myself I **could figure it out**! |
|---|---|---|

And when you finished the eight mathematics problems, how confident did you feel about your work? Did you feel confident you reached a reasonable solution? Did you feel confident that you did not reach a reasonable solution, but you knew where the issue lay? Or did you feel exasperated that there was no answer key in the back of the book? Where would you place your feeling along this continuum?

_____

_____

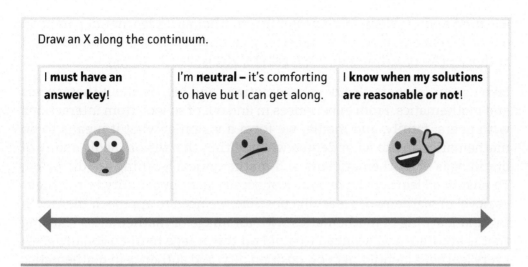

Draw an X along the continuum.

| I **must have an answer key!** | I'm **neutral** – it's comforting to have but I can get along. | I **know when my solutions are reasonable or not!** |

**Image source:** istock.com/calvindexter

Let's dig a little deeper. Ask yourself why. Whether you said, "I am afraid of math!" or "I love thinking and learning about math!" or something in between, verbalize why. Write a list of whys near your emoji or face.

Next, consider why you reacted to those eight mathematics problems the way you did. Why did you feel like you could *not* do them, or why did you feel like you could? Write this list of whys near your emoji or face on the second continuum.

Then, reflect on why you felt the way you did when you got stuck or struggled. Why did you feel like giving up? Or why did you feel like you could figure it out? Write this list of whys near your emoji or face on the third continuum.

Finally, think back to why you felt the way you did at the end of working on the problems. Why did you immediately search for an answer key? Or why were you content with wherever you landed with each problem? Write this list of whys near your emoji or face on the last continuum.

Putting your whys into words requires honesty and vulnerability. Thank you. We'll return to these lists later in this module.

Each continuum represents a facet of being a mathematical learner. First, we reflected on our **identity** as mathematics learners: How do we see ourselves as doers and knowers of mathematics? This often translates as follows: How do we feel about mathematics? Next, we reflected on our **positionality** as mathematics learners: How do the mathematics problems and the presentation of the problems communicate our position as mathematicians? Are we situated as competent and necessary members of our learning community or as incompetent and outsiders? And as a result, do we believe we can do it? Next, we reflected on our **agency** as mathematics learners: To what degree do we activate our initiative, self-regulation, and problem solving when engaged in mathematics? And finally, we reflected on our **authority** as mathematics learners: To what degree do we share authority as sense makers of mathematics and active decision makers who own our learning and problem solving? Being a mathematics learner depends on our development of positive and strong identity, agency, positionality, and authority (Berry & Thunder, 2012; NCTM, 2020a, 2020b, 2020c).

Like us, our learners also develop emotions and beliefs about themselves and mathematics. From experiences in and out of school, from interactions with peers, family, and media, we form a vision of what it means to do mathematics and to what degree we fit within that vision. Sadly, many of our images of mathematicians and mathematical learning are distorted. To ensure *all* learners have equity of access and opportunity to the highest level of mathematics learning possible, we need to approach the teaching and learning of mathematics with an image of mathematics learning that is accurate and we need to build on this image to intentionally grow every learner's identity, agency, positionality, and authority in mathematics (Berry & Thunder, 2012; NCTM, 2020a, 2020b, 2020c).

# MODULE #4

### Learning Intention

We are learning about the significance of developing identity, agency, positionality, and authority as mathematics learners so that we can broaden the pathway of mathematics learning for all learners.

### Success Criteria

We'll know we've learned this when we can:

1. redefine what it means to be a mathematician in ways that reflect the real work of mathematicians,

2. describe the six characteristics of students who drive their own mathematics learning,

3. develop a vision of a mathematics learner that aligns with being a mathematician and driving mathematics learning, and

4. recognize opportunities to develop the qualities of a mathematician and driving mathematics learning in standards and curricular documents.

## BEING A MATHEMATICIAN

Our mathematics teaching must integrate all aspects of "what it means to learn mathematics." Just as an apprentice deliberately practices the craft they learn, we must engage in the authentic processes and practices, or the ways of working and thinking, of mathematicians in order to be mathematical learners and to develop a positive identity as a mathematics learner. In other words, we need to know what it means to be a mathematician and our mathematics teaching and learning should reflect this.

Look back at your lists of whys along the four continua. Within these whys, some words describe the qualities of a mathematician and the work of a mathematician. It may be that you see these qualities in yourself. Or it may be that you see opposite qualities or a lack of these qualities in yourself. It may be that you identify with the work, or maybe you don't. Take a moment to record below the qualities of a mathematician.

A mathematician is/can . . .

_____

_____

_____

_____

Now, let's compare our images of mathematicians with how mathematicians describe themselves and their work. Below are four quotes from mathematicians. As you read each quote, highlight, circle, or underline words and phrases that stand out to you perhaps because they affirm your vision or perhaps because they contradict it.

A mathematician, like a painter or a poet, is a maker of patterns.

**— G. H. Hardy, mathematician & mentor of mathematicians**

Everyone knows that it is easy to do a puzzle if someone has told you the answer. That is simply a test of memory. You can claim to be a mathematician only if you can solve puzzles that you have never studied before. That is the test of reasoning.

**— W. W. Sawyer, mathematician & mathematics educator**

Do the research. Ask questions. Find someone doing what you are interested in! Be curious! I like to learn. That's an art and a science.

**— Katherine Johnson, mathematician for NASA**

Mathematicians like me often teach math as if we know everything. The truth, which we reveal to our students too rarely, is that we know almost nothing. One step outside the lighted circle of the understood, and everything is unmapped wilderness. A lot of people find this unsettling. For Urschel, it was thrilling. "It was *so hard*," he told me. "And it was a struggle that I really loved."

The world thinks mathematicians are people for whom math is easy. That's wrong. Sure, some kids, like Urschel, have little trouble with school math. But everyone who starts down the road to creating really new mathematics finds out what Urschel did: It's a struggle. A prickly, sometimes lonely struggle whose rewards are uncertain and a long time coming. Mathematicians are the people who love that struggle.

**— Jordan Ellenberg about his interview with fellow mathematician and former NFL player, John Urschel**

Look back at your description of the qualities of a mathematician and the work of a mathematician. How do these quotes compare with your description? Make additions, deletions, and revisions to your current definition of a mathematician.

We recognize that every learner may not seek future employment as a mathematician or work in an applied mathematics field, like engineering, finance, or computer science. But every learner deserves the opportunity and access to mathematical teaching and learning that empowers them to make that decision for themselves. When we ensure that our schools and classrooms integrate all aspects of "what it means to learn mathematics," then we change mathematics from a gatekeeper to a broad gateway for all learners.

---

Another way to examine what it truly means to be a mathematician is to examine the significance of relational understanding and the five elements of mathematical understanding for thinking about and doing mathematics. We first introduced these concepts in Module #1. Let's recall that information.

In your words, what is **relational understanding**?

_____

_____

What are **the five elements of mathematical understanding**?

1. _____

2. _____

3. _____

4. _____

5. _____

If you need help recalling, flip back to pp. 20–27.

---

We can make each of these understandings into statements about mathematicians' ways of working and thinking: Mathematicians understand the why behind what they do. Mathematicians know and make connections among concepts. They are fluent decision-makers with procedures. They transfer, generalize, and apply strategies. Mathematicians reason about novel and truly problematic situations. They hold productive dispositions, like believing they are up to the challenge. These statements communicate positive identity, agency, positionality, and authority as mathematicians.

Let's return to your definition of a mathematician on p. 67 in this module. How does your definition encompass the elements of mathematical understanding? Take a moment and return to that definition. Mark your responses based on the element of mathematics understanding represented in your responses. Use the following key to complete the task:

- Put a **C** next to those responses that represent conceptual knowledge.

- Put a **P** next to those responses that represent procedural fluency.

- Put an **S** next to those responses that represent strategic competence.

- Put an **A** next to those responses that represent adaptive reasoning.

- Put a **D** next to those responses that represent productive dispositions.

If you have statements that are contradictory to these understandings, delete them. If you are missing any of these understandings, add them. You may also want to revise your language to be more precise or to be clearer. Make additions, deletions, and revisions to your definition based on the elements of mathematical understanding.

Our vision of what it means to truly be a mathematician and engage in thinking about and doing mathematics is becoming clearer and more accurate. How is this reflected in our mathematics standards and supporting documents? Most mathematics state standards emphasize not only the proficiencies of mathematicians but also their practices and processes. In other words, they describe the positive identity, agency, positionality, and authority of mathematics learners. Let's look at three states' standards where these practices and processes are explicitly called out.

- Take a look at Figure 4.1, the mathematics practice standards from Georgia (Georgia Department of Education, 2021).

**FIGURE 4.1** ● Mathematics practice standards from Georgia.

| MATHEMATICAL PRACTICES | |
|---|---|
| **MP:** Display perseverance and patience in problem-solving. Demonstrate skills and strategies needed to succeed in mathematics, including critical thinking, reasoning, and effective collaboration and expression. Seek help and apply feedback. Set and monitor goals. | |
| **CODE** | **EXPECTATION** |
| **MP.1** | Make sense of problems and persevere in solving them. |
| **MP.2** | Reason abstractly and quantitatively. |

*(Continued)*

(Continued)

| CODE | EXPECTATION |
|------|-------------|
| MP.3 | Construct viable arguments and critique the reasoning of others. |
| MP.4 | Model with mathematics. |
| MP.5 | Use appropriate tools strategically. |
| MP.6 | Attend to precision. |
| MP.7 | Look for and make use of structure. |
| MP.8 | Look for and express regularity in repeated reasoning. |

**Source:** Georgia Department of Education (2021).

- Take a look at Figure 4.2, the mathematics process standards from Texas (Texas Education Agency, Texas Essential Knowledge and Skills for Mathematics, 2015).

**FIGURE 4.2** ● Mathematics process standards from Texas.

Mathematical process standards. The student uses mathematical processes to acquire and demonstrate mathematical understanding. The student is expected to:

(A) apply mathematics to problems arising in everyday life, society, and the workplace;

(B) use a problem-solving model that incorporates analyzing given information, formulating a plan or strategy, determining a solution, justifying the solution, and evaluating the problem-solving process and the reasonableness of the solution;

(C) select tools, including real objects, manipulatives, paper and pencil, and technology as appropriate, and techniques, including mental math, estimation, and number sense as appropriate, to solve problems;

(D) communicate mathematical ideas, reasoning, and their implications using multiple representations, including symbols, diagrams, graphs, and language as appropriate;

(E) create and use representations to organize, record, and communicate mathematical ideas;

(F) analyze mathematical relationships to connect and communicate mathematical ideas; and

(G) display, explain, and justify mathematical ideas and arguments using precise mathematical language in written or oral communication.

**Source:** Texas Education Agency (2015).

- And finally, take a look at Figure 4.3, the mathematics process goals from Virginia (Virginia Board of Education, Mathematics Standards of Learning for Virginia Public Schools, K–12, 2016):

**FIGURE 4.3** ● Mathematics process goals from Virginia.

**Mathematical Problem Solving**

Students will apply mathematical concepts and skills and the relationships among them to solve problem situations of varying complexities. Students also will recognize and create problems from real-world data and situations within and outside mathematics and then apply appropriate strategies to determine acceptable solutions. To accomplish this goal, students will need to develop a repertoire of skills and strategies for solving a variety of problem types. A major goal of the mathematics program is to help students apply mathematics concepts and skills to become mathematical problem solvers.

**Mathematical Communication**

Students will communicate thinking and reasoning using the language of mathematics, including specialized vocabulary and symbolic notation, to express mathematical ideas with precision. Representing, discussing, justifying, conjecturing, reading, writing, presenting, and listening to mathematics will help students to clarify their thinking and deepen their understanding of the mathematics being studied. Mathematical communication becomes visible where learning involves participation in mathematical discussions.

**Mathematical Reasoning**

Students will recognize reasoning and proof as fundamental aspects of mathematics. Students will learn and apply inductive and deductive reasoning skills to make, test, and evaluate mathematical statements and to justify steps in mathematical procedures. Students will use logical reasoning to analyze an argument and to determine whether conclusions are valid. In addition, students will use number sense to apply proportional and spatial reasoning and to reason from a variety of representations.

**Mathematical Connections**

Students will build upon prior knowledge to relate concepts and procedures from different topics within mathematics and see mathematics as an integrated field of study. Through the practical application of content and process skills, students will make connections among different areas of mathematics and between mathematics and other disciplines, and to real-world contexts. Science and mathematics teachers and curriculum writers are encouraged to develop mathematics and science curricula that support, apply, and reinforce each other.

**Mathematical Representations**

Students will represent and describe mathematical ideas, generalizations, and relationships using a variety of methods. Students will understand that representations of mathematical ideas are an essential part of learning, doing, and communicating mathematics. Students should make connections among different representations – physical, visual, symbolic, verbal, and contextual – and recognize that representation is both a process and a product.

**Source:** Virginia Board of Education (2016).

Choose one set of practice or process standards to analyze. Using a highlighter or colorful writing utensil, identify when the practice or process standards align with your definition of a mathematician.

How do these practice and process standards emphasize the real work of being a mathematician? Where do you see characteristics of mathematics learners' identity, agency, positionality, and authority? We have provided our analysis of the Texas mathematics process standards below for reference and as an example.

**FIGURE 4.4** ● Texas mathematics process standards analysis.

Mathematical process standards. The student uses mathematical processes to acquire and demonstrate mathematical understanding. The student is expected to:

(A) apply mathematics to problems arising in everyday life, society, and the workplace;

(B) use a problem-solving model that incorporates analyzing given information, formulating a plan or strategy, determining a solution, justifying the solution, and evaluating the problem-solving process and the reasonableness of the solution;

(C) select tools, including real objects, manipulatives, paper and pencil, and technology as appropriate, and techniques, including mental math, estimation, and number sense as appropriate, to solve problems;

(D) communicate mathematical ideas, reasoning, and their implications using multiple representations, including symbols, diagrams, graphs, and language as appropriate;

(E) create and use representations to organize, record, and communicate mathematical ideas;

(F) analyze mathematical relationships to connect and communicate mathematical ideas; and

(G) display, explain, and justify mathematical ideas and arguments using precise mathematical language in written or oral communication.

**Source:** Adapted from Texas Education Agency (2015).

Return to your definition of a mathematician one more time. Make additions, deletions, and revisions. You may also want to look at your state standards to see how they describe the practices and processes of mathematicians.

Whatever definition of a mathematician you have landed on, we hope the thing we all have in common across our definitions is a realization that being a mathematician is much more than providing "the right answer," following an algorithm, replicating solutions to problems that have already been solved, and knowing how to solve every problem. Being a mathematician is about sense making. So many active, powerful verbs describe the work of "what it means to learn mathematics." Our mathematics teaching must integrate all aspects of this so that all learners have equitable access and opportunity to the highest levels of mathematics. Every learner deserves positive and strong identity, agency, positionality, and authority as a mathematics learner.

Our mathematics teaching must foster, nurture, and sustain learners who own their learning of mathematics. We must empower every learner to see themselves as mathematics learners. In other words, we must develop students who drive their own mathematics learning.

## DRIVING THEIR OWN MATHEMATICS LEARNING

Every learner should have equity of access and opportunity to the highest level of mathematics learning possible. To achieve this, we must intentionally grow every student's identity, agency, positionality, and authority specifically as mathematics learners but also simply as learners. How do our learners define learning, and how do they **identify** with these images? How do we **position** each learner as critical and competent within the learning community? How do we empower our learners with **agency** to initiate, self-monitor, and problem solve about their learning? And how do we empower our learners with shared **authority** to self-evaluate and own their learning journeys?

We create a cohesive experience for learners when we focus on developing identity, agency, positionality, and authority around the proficiencies, processes, and practices of learners regardless of the subject area. The six characteristics of students who drive their own learning resonate across subject areas, across ages, and throughout our lifelong paths as learners. Students who drive their own learning:

- know their current level of understanding; they can communicate what they do and do not yet know,

- know where they are going next in their learning and are ready to take on the challenge,

- select tools to move their learning and development forward,

- seek feedback about their learning and recognize errors as opportunities to learn,

- monitor their learning and make adjustments when necessary, and

- recognize when they have learned something and serve as a teacher to others (Fisher et al., 2023).

These characteristics students who drive their own learning provide us with the criteria to measure our success in developing identity, agency, positionality, and authority in our learners.

Let's return to your description of the qualities of a mathematician and the work of a mathematician. Driving learning and being a mathematics learner intersect. In the second column of the table below, pull statements from your definition of a mathematician and place them next to the aligning characteristic of a student who drives their own learning. For example, if you said, "Mathematicians love the struggle," you might record that statement in the same row as the characteristic of students who drive their own learning: "Recognize errors as opportunities to learn."

| STUDENTS WHO DRIVE THEIR OWN LEARNING | MATHEMATICIANS | MATHEMATICAL PRACTICE OR PROCESS STANDARDS |
|---|---|---|
| Know their current level of understanding; they can communicate what they do and do not yet know. | | |
| Know where they are going next in their learning and are ready to take on the challenge. | | |
| Select tools to move their learning and development forward. | | |
| Seek feedback about their learning and recognize errors as opportunities to learn. | | |
| Monitor their learning and make adjustments when necessary. | | |
| Recognize when they have learned something and serve as a teacher to others. | | |

Next, let's look back at the practice or process standards that you analyzed on pp. 69–71. Driving learning and the expectations for the practices and process of a mathematics learner intersect. In the third column of the table above, pull statements from that set of standards and place them next to the aligning characteristic of students who drive their own learning. For example, we previously highlighted, "Evaluating the problem-solving process and the reasonableness of the solution," so we would record that statement in the same row as the characteristic of students who drive their own learning: "Monitor their learning and make adjustments when necessary."

## BEING A MATHEMATICS LEARNER IN MY CLASSROOM

What does it mean to learn mathematics? What does it mean to be a mathematics learner in your classroom?

If you were to make a slogan for your classroom or post a welcome sign to reference throughout the year, if you were to share this statement with every learner, every family member, every visitor to your classroom, what would you say in one to two sentences? We'll help get you started:

*Being a mathematics learner means . . .*

_____

_____

_____

_____

To teach and learn mathematics, we must have a clear, accurate vision of mathematics learners. And then we need to use this vision to inform the ways we engage our learners in learning mathematics. The identity, agency, positionality, and authority of every learner matters so that every learner has the equity of access and opportunity to the highest levels of mathematics learning.

# Exit Ticket

Take a moment and self-evaluate your learning in this module using these statements.

1. I can redefine what it means to be a mathematician in ways that reflect the real work of mathematicians.

| 1 | 2 | 3 | 4 | 5 |
|---|---|---|---|---|
| Strongly disagree | Disagree | Neutral | Agree | Strongly agree |

Explain the reason for your selection.

_____

_____

2. I can describe the six characteristics of students who drive their own mathematics learning.

| 1 | 2 | 3 | 4 | 5 |
|---|---|---|---|---|
| Strongly disagree | Disagree | Neutral | Agree | Strongly agree |

Explain the reason for your selection.

_____

_____

3. I can develop a vision of a mathematics learner that aligns with being a mathematician and being a student who drives their own mathematics learning.

| 1 | 2 | 3 | 4 | 5 |
|---|---|---|---|---|
| Strongly disagree | Disagree | Neutral | Agree | Strongly agree |

Explain the reason for your selection.

_____

_____

4. I can recognize opportunities to develop the qualities of a mathematician and a student who drives their own mathematics learning in standards and curricular documents.

| 1 | 2 | 3 | 4 | 5 |
|---|---|---|---|---|
| Strongly disagree | Disagree | Neutral | Agree | Strongly agree |

Explain the reason for your selection.

_____

_____

# What Is an *Engaged* Mathematics Learner?

When students enter your classroom, despite whether your students identify as mathematicians and learners, they must be engaged to move their mathematical learning forward. So what does it mean to be engaged? And how do we foster engagement in our mathematics classrooms? In future modules, we'll examine mathematics tasks, mathematics talk, and other teaching moves to engage learners in mathematics concepts and skills. But in this module, we look closely at what it means to be engaged as a learner and how we can shift the ownership of engagement to our learners. We want our learners to be empowered to actively engage. In other words, we want our leaners to drive their own mathematical learning.

## MODULE #5

**Learning Intention**

We are learning what it means to be engaged in mathematics learning so that we can empower our students to drive their learning.

**Success Criteria**

We'll know we've learned this when we can:

1. describe indicators of engagement and disengagement as a mathematics learner,

2. identify ways to foster engagement through our intentional decisions about mathematics teaching and learning, and

3. recognize opportunities to partner with learners and empower them as engaged mathematics learners.

When we began this Playbook, you made a list of wonderings and challenges (see p. 2). Kateri often wondered about engaging learners. At times, engagement in her classroom felt like the tide: something that ebbed and flowed, happened or didn't, and was beyond her control. Kateri got a mixed bag of advice about increasing learners' engagement with two frequent messages: Engagement is about classroom management or engagement is about fun. It wasn't until Kateri's instructional coach documented her instructional moves in tandem with her learners' engagement that she realized engagement is about intentional teaching and learning by both the teacher and the learners.

As educators and as a learning community, we can and should intentionally engage learners. When we do this, we maximize the potential impact of teaching and learning. But we can't stop there. Our school, our classroom, and ourselves as teachers won't always be present to intentionally engage learners. On some days, our learners will have a substitute teacher. At the end of the mathematics period, our learners may have another teacher for history, art, physical education, or world languages. And at the end of the school year, our learners will move onto new mathematics classes with other teachers. Eventually, our learners will be adult learners, who may want to learn new hobbies, languages, or job skills. We can and should intentionally shift the ownership of learners' engagement to the learner and empower each individual to make intentional decisions to engage in learning. When we do this, we inspire learners to maximize the potential impact of teaching and learning and become students who drive their own mathematics learning.

Let's look back at the characteristics of students who drive their own mathematics learning. Within each characteristic, there are things we must do intentionally so that learners can demonstrate the characteristic. And there are things learners must do for themselves to demonstrate the characteristic. Take a moment to read each characteristic and identify the intentional work of teachers and learners so that learners can drive their own mathematics learning.

| STUDENTS WHO DRIVE THEIR OWN LEARNING | AS TEACHERS, WE MUST INTENTIONALLY... | SO THAT LEARNERS CAN INTENTIONALLY... |
|---|---|---|
| Know their current level of understanding; they can communicate what they do and do not yet know. | | |
| Know where they are going next in their learning and are ready to take on the challenge. | | |
| Select tools to move their learning and development forward. | | |

| STUDENTS WHO DRIVE THEIR OWN LEARNING | AS TEACHERS, WE MUST INTENTIONALLY... | SO THAT LEARNERS CAN INTENTIONALLY... |
|---|---|---|
| Seek feedback about their learning and recognize errors as opportunities to learn. | | |
| Monitor their learning and make adjustments when necessary. | | |
| Recognize when they have learned something and serve as a teacher to others. | | |

Now that we see where we're headed, let's dig deeper into ways to intentionally engage our learners.

## WHAT DOES IT MEAN TO BE ENGAGED AS A LEARNER?

You've probably heard advice about engagement and have noticed some indicators of engagement and disengagement in your mathematics class. Let's make a list of those indicators.

| WHAT DO YOU SEE AND HEAR THAT LETS YOU KNOW YOUR LEARNERS ARE ENGAGED? | WHAT DO YOU SEE AND HEAR THAT LETS YOU KNOW YOUR LEARNERS ARE DISENGAGED? |
|---|---|
| _____ | _____ |
| _____ | _____ |
| _____ | _____ |
| _____ | _____ |

Engagement is like a soundboard, which relies on multiple input signals that can be adjusted and merged together. Each input signal is controlled by a channel of knobs that shape, amplify, and split the input sounds. There are four dimensions of school engagement: behavioral, cognitive, affective, and social (Fredricks et al., 2004; Wang et al., 2019).

**4 Dimensions of School Engagement**

| BEHAVIORAL ENGAGEMENT | COGNITIVE ENGAGEMENT | AFFECTIVE ENGAGEMENT | SOCIAL ENGAGEMENT |
|---|---|---|---|
| Engaging in learning activities | Investment in learning | Feeling of belonging | Quality of social interactions |

- **Behavioral Engagement** is a learner's productive and proactive participation in both learning and nonlearning activities at school. There are three main indicator categories: conduct, academic, and participation. Conduct indicators show learners follow the rules and established norms and in general do what is expected to be successful. Academic indicators show learners demonstrate academic behaviors for learning, such as putting forth effort, paying attention, and asking questions. Participation indicators show learners take part in school or class events and activities.

- **Cognitive Engagement** is a learner's investment in learning. There are two main indicator categories: psychological investment and strategic investment. Psychological investment is the desire to learn as much as possible and the willingness to go beyond minimal requirements to demonstrate mastery. Strategic investments are the functional strategies learners use to invest in the process of learning, such as planning, studying, and organizing, as well as the investment in goals that are the outcome of learning, such as grades, post–high-school placements, and job opportunities.

- **Affective Engagement** is a learner's feeling of belonging. There are two main indicator categories: feelings and emotional connections. A learner's feelings about experiences can reflect the specific moment, as well as an accumulation of feelings about experiences with mathematics, learning in class, and the school. A learner's emotional connections encompass connectivity and belonging within the mathematics class, with the mathematics teacher, among mathematics classmates, as well as in school, at school events, and with other school personnel and peers.

- **Social Engagement** is a learner's quality of social interactions in the learning process. Learning does not happen in isolation. It happens through the accumulation of interactions between learners and teachers, shaping the experiences in the classroom.

Learners can simultaneously demonstrate both engagement and disengagement within each dimension and across dimensions. On our engagement "soundboard," there are channels for behavioral engagement and for behavioral disengagement, for cognitive engagement and for cognitive disengagement, and so on. In other words, learners may never be 100% engaged or 100% disengaged at school, but they will demonstrate indicators of both engagement and disengagement, in different or similar ways, across their school day and in each school space. Each dimension is equally important to engagement in learning. Just as the soundboard merges all input signals together to create a cohesive audio recording, the portrait of a learner's engagement encompasses the whole multidimensional framework of engagement.

Are you starting to see yourself or specific learners described within these dimensions and indicators? We certainly are. Here is an example from Kateri's reflection:

> As a high school mathematics learner, Kateri followed the mathematics class rules but chose not to participate in whole class discussions. She invested a lot of time in studying for mathematics tests and was very organized taking notes in mathematics class, but she did the minimum to earn her desired score on mathematics assignments and projects. Kateri had many positive feelings about mathematical learning and persevered through challenging tasks, but she did not feel connected to certain mathematics classes, and as a result, she often skipped those. She recalls earning As on her report cards with teacher comments like "would do better if attended class regularly." The quality of Kateri's social interactions in mathematics class also varied. Opportunities to tutor a peer were often high-quality social interactions for her, while working in an assigned small group was often low quality. Kateri demonstrated similar and different indicators of both engagement and disengagement in other subject areas and in other nonlearning school spaces, including lunch, clubs, assemblies, and sports.

Choose a time period from your life: early childhood, elementary, middle, or high school.

| HOW WOULD YOU DESCRIBE YOUR ENGAGEMENT AS A MATHEMATICS LEARNER ACROSS EACH DIMENSION? | HOW WOULD YOUR MATHEMATICS TEACHER DESCRIBE YOUR ENGAGEMENT AS A MATHEMATICS LEARNER ACROSS EACH DIMENSION? |
|---|---|
| _____ | _____ |
| _____ | _____ |
| _____ | _____ |
| _____ | _____ |

**Compare your reflections:** What indicators of engagement or disengagement did you identify? How might your appearances have been aligned or misaligned with your actual engagement?

_____

_____

_____

_____

Think about a specific learner in your mathematics class.

| WHAT SIGNS OF ENGAGEMENT DO YOU NOTICE? | WHAT SIGNS OF DISENGAGEMENT DO YOU NOTICE? |
|---|---|
| _____ | _____ |
| _____ | _____ |
| _____ | _____ |
| _____ | _____ |

**Compare your reflections:** What indicators of engagement or disengagement did you identify? How might your learner's appearances indicate or distract you from their actual engagement?

_____

_____

_____

_____

We need to pause here to both realize and appreciate that our perceptions of learners' engagement and their actual engagement do not always align. Engagement is not an all-or-nothing characteristic. As we saw in Kateri's reflection, learners can display both indications of being engaged and disengaged at the same time. Similarly, we may misinterpret a learner's actions and language as a sign of engagement or disengagement.

For example, we reflected on a learner in our mathematics class who often "calls out" and "disrupts" the flow of class discourse. But when we listen more closely to what the learner is saying, we realize these disruptions are actually the learner participating and sharing mathematical ideas in a pattern of group discourse that reflects the way a group of friends or family may talk with many voices overlapping. This learner demonstrates signs of behavioral and cognitive engagement, although some educators might perceive the learner as "disrupting."

Another learner appears highly engaged when working independently on mathematics tasks that require quick answers with little effort or investment in the process. At first glance, we perceived this "on-task" behavior as engagement. But looking deeper, the learner complied with certain tasks while avoiding collaborative tasks and refused to engage in tasks that required in-depth thinking and effort. This learner demonstrates signs of cognitive and social disengagement, although some educators might perceive the learner as "focused."

This is the reality of engagement. Engagement is an accumulation of traits. It is complex and dynamic. In some ways, engagement may ebb and flow like the tide, but it's never beyond our control. Some aspects of engagement are related to classroom management, and some aspects are about having fun. But engagement is more than just behavior and fun. It is multidimensional. Learners' engagement depends on our intentional teaching and learning.

## HOW CAN WE INTENTIONALLY ENGAGE LEARNERS?

When we create a mathematics learning community that fosters behavioral, cognitive, affective, and social engagement, we maximize the potential impact of teaching and learning. With these dimensions of engagement in mind, we can make intentional decisions to engage all learners in mathematics teaching and learning. We can take action each day to engage learners across the four dimensions.

When we make intentional plans for engagement, we should also consider individuals, as well as our class as a whole. What is engaging for one learner may be disengaging for another. This demands that we use a variety of instructional strategies to engage our learners. Our four big ideas for mathematical teaching and learning offer us ways to create cohesive and engaging experiences for our learners that are flexible enough to connect with all our learners.

Let's consider the ways our four big ideas could foster engagement across the four dimensions. In the tables below, finish each statement to identify ways the big ideas help us develop and protect engagement in each dimension. Some of our ideas are included below to support your brainstorming.

## BIG IDEA #1

When our mathematics teaching integrates all aspects of "what it means to learn mathematics," we develop and protect . . .

| behavioral engagement because . . . | cognitive engagement because . . . | affective engagement because . . . | social engagement because . . . |
|---|---|---|---|
| | | *the definition of what it means to be a mathematician and/or a learner can be wide enough to include all learners and allow everyone to experience a sense of belonging.* | |

## BIG IDEA #2

When the expectations for mathematics learning are clearly shared with and communicated to our learners, we develop and protect . . .

| behavioral engagement because . . . | cognitive engagement because . . . | affective engagement because . . . | social engagement because . . . |
|---|---|---|---|
| | | | *we can intentionally teach learners ways to effectively collaborate, debate, and share ideas.* |

# BIG IDEA #3

When mathematics teaching and learning is reflected in rigorous mathematical experiences and tasks, we develop and protect . . .

| behavioral engagement because . . . | cognitive engagement because . . . | affective engagement because . . . | social engagement because . . . |
|---|---|---|---|
| *sense making, problem solving, persistence, and reasoning are explicitly practiced and valued through these types of tasks.* | | | |

# BIG IDEA #4

When mathematics teaching and learning require and depend on the generation and interpretation of evidence, we develop and protect . . .

| behavioral engagement because . . . | cognitive engagement because . . . | affective engagement because . . . | social engagement because . . . |
|---|---|---|---|
| | *we examine the three-dimensional evidence of mastery for elements of mathematical teaching and learning, beyond flat measures such as attendance and grades.* | | |

This work to intentionally engage our mathematics learners is worth our time and effort. We must keep the whole portrait of an engaged learner in mind as we intentionally implement and adjust our instruction and interactions to maximize the impact of mathematics teaching and learning. We must also foster the transfer of engagement across settings over time. The one constant is the learner, so we need to shift the ownership of engagement to our learners.

## HOW CAN WE EMPOWER OUR LEARNERS TO OWN THEIR ENGAGEMENT?

We want learners to make intentional decisions to engage in learning while they are learning with us and beyond. This transfer toward self-regulation of engagement requires that we work in partnership with our learners to find out what engages and disengages them, how they demonstrate engagement and disengagement, and what strategies they have to advocate for, invest in, and drive their own learning.

The school engagement framework can serve as a tool to inform and support our partnerships with learners about engagement. First, we need to grow learners' awareness of the dimensions of engagement and their habits for demonstrating engagement and disengagement. Then, we can partner with learners to notice patterns in what engages and disengages them. And finally, we can lean on the framework as a tool for feedback about engagement. As teachers, we can engage in conversations to provide learners with feedback about their engagement. Learners can use their growing awareness and reflections to self-monitor their engagement, as well as to generate and interpret evidence of their engagement. And peers can rely on the framework to provide feedback to each other. We will dive more deeply into feedback in Module #14 and into evidence generation and interpretation in Module #12 and Module #13.

Most frequently, learners receive feedback about their engagement through grades and behavioral consequences. These two pieces of engagement evidence are flawed. To truly empower learners to own their engagement across learning experiences, we need to rethink the ways learners receive engagement feedback. How can we make engagement feedback learner friendly, actionable, and a bite-sized chunk of information? How can engagement feedback reflect the complex and dynamic nature of engagement? Creating norms or a classroom pact as a learning community is one way to begin this partnership, especially when the norms encompass behavioral, cognitive, affective, and social engagement.

Here are some examples of protocols mathematics teachers have used to create norms, to reflect on engagement and disengagement, and to partner with learners about engagement:

**Start/Stop Protocol**

To maximize my learning through my engagement,

| What should I START doing? | What should I STOP doing? |
|---|---|
| What should I NOT STOP doing? | What should I NOT START doing? |

*What do you notice about this protocol?*

*How does this protocol reflect the four dimensions of engagement?*

*How could you use this protocol to partner with learners about engagement?*

---

**Individual and Collective Learning Protocol**

| What do **I do** to make this an effective learning experience **for myself?** | What do **I do** to make this an effective learning experience **for others?** |
|---|---|

*What do you notice about this protocol?*

*How does this protocol reflect the four dimensions of engagement?*

*How could you use this protocol to partner with learners about engagement?*

---

**Rights of Learners Protocol**

- the right to be confused

- the right to make a mistake

- the right to say what makes sense to you

- the right to share unfinished thinking and not be judged

- the right to revise your thinking

(Kalinec-Craig, 2017)

*Which "right" most resonates with you? Why? If you're stuck, try thinking about which one hurts the most if it is violated.*

*What does it look and sound like to **exercise your rights**?*

*What does it look and sound like to **advocate for your peers' rights**?*

*What do you notice about this protocol?*

*How does this protocol reflect the four dimensions of engagement?*

*How could you use this protocol to partner with learners about engagement?*

---

These norms must become living documents through deliberate teaching and learning about enacting the norms. In other words, the norms should inform the language and social learning intentions, as well as the success criteria of daily learning.

# Exit Ticket

Take a moment and self-evaluate your learning in this module using these statements.

1. I can describe indicators of engagement and disengagement as a mathematics learner.

| 1 | 2 | 3 | 4 | 5 |
|---|---|---|---|---|
| Strongly disagree | Disagree | Neutral | Agree | Strongly agree |

Explain the reason for your selection.

_____

_____

2. I can identify ways to foster engagement through my intentional decisions about mathematics teaching and learning.

| 1 | 2 | 3 | 4 | 5 |
|---|---|---|---|---|
| Strongly disagree | Disagree | Neutral | Agree | Strongly agree |

Explain the reason for your selection.

_____

_____

3. I can recognize opportunities to partner with learners and empower them as engaged mathematics learners.

| 1 | 2 | 3 | 4 | 5 |
|---|---|---|---|---|
| Strongly disagree | Disagree | Neutral | Agree | Strongly agree |

Explain the reason for your selection.

_____

_____

# What Are the Misalignments, Misconceptions, and Missed Opportunities in Mathematical Learning and Engagement?

One of the purposes of this Playbook is to create an intentional space for engaging in critical dialogue, addressing impactful issues, making sense of the growing body of educational research, and moving from research to reality. In this module, we make room for critical conversations that make sense of the misalignments, misconceptions, and missed opportunities in mathematical learning and engagement.

This module demands that we are not only open to changing and improving our practices but also that we are ready to take action to reframe, respond to, and revolutionize the critical challenges of learning and engagement in mathematics. As you read the learning intentions, relevance, and success criteria for this module, take note of the verbs in the success criteria. Each pair of verbs reflects this focus to intentionally become aware *and* shift to action.

# MODULE #6

**Learning Intention**

We are learning about the misalignments, misconceptions, and missed opportunities in mathematical learning and engagement so that we can ensure *all* learners have equity of access and opportunity to the highest level of mathematics learning possible.

**Success Criteria**

We'll know we've learned this when we can:

1. identify and revolutionize mathematical teaching practices when the intent is misaligned with the impact;

2. examine and pursue the missed opportunities for mathematical learning and engagement when we narrow and restrict who can do mathematics, what mathematics is, and how mathematics and mathematics learning work; and

3. explain and reframe misconceptions about mathematical learning and engagement that impact our decision-making and teaching practices and, therefore, impact our students' learning.

---

There are numerous ways to conceive of and represent the many pieces of mathematics learning and engagement. Since this is a *mathematics* playbook, let's try an equation. What are the essential components or variables that combine to create learning and engagement in mathematics? What might your equation include?

_____

_____

_____

_____

---

Here is an equation that we created to represent one way we think about the essential variables that contribute to learning and engagement in mathematics:

$$\text{learners} + \text{mathematics} + \text{connections} + \text{our decisions and practices} = \text{learning and engagement in mathematics}$$

We keep our eyes relentlessly on the learning of our students and on the impact of our decisions and teaching practices on *every* learner. When we narrow and restrict *who* can do mathematics, we remove the learner from the equation and create inequity in mathematical learning and engagement. When we narrow and restrict *what* mathematics is, we remove the real mathematics from the equation and create inaccuracies in mathematical learning and engagement. When we narrow and restrict *how* mathematics and mathematical learning work, we remove the meaningful connections from the equation and create incoherence in mathematical learning and engagement. Let's unpack these misalignments, misconceptions, and missed opportunities and examine the research to revolutionize our decision-making and teaching practices.

## MATHEMATICS IS A HUMAN ENDEAVOR

Have you heard people proclaim, "I'm not a math person" or "I don't do math"? Maybe you've even said this yourself. Others sometimes hold their interest or skill in mathematics with a degree of elitism, as though being good at mathematics or liking mathematics is a special club for members only. Maybe you feel this way too, and this feeling is reinforced when you're told your strengths and positive attitude toward mathematics are unique.

These two opposing dispositions give the illusion that there are two kinds of people in the world—those who can do mathematics and those who can't. But really there are just people. And *all* people do mathematics because mathematics is a human endeavor. Counting, calculating, measuring, noticing patterns, collecting and analyzing data, categorizing, and representing are all the daily work of being a person in the world.

When we make decisions and teach from the false dichotomy, we may intend to meet the needs of diverse learners, but the impact does not align with the intent.

Let's look at examples of mathematics teaching practices when the intent of the practice does not align with the impact of the practice. Begin by reflecting on why you have put these practices into action or what you've heard from others as they explain their decision-making process.

| TEACHING PRACTICE | DEFINITION | WHAT IS THE INTENT OF THE TEACHING PRACTICE? (WHY IS THIS PRACTICE PUT INTO ACTION?) |
|---|---|---|
| Tracking | Separating students, most often by academic ability, into groups for mathematics, and often then adjusting the expanse and depth of the mathematics curriculum for these tracks. | |

*(Continued)*

(Continued)

| TEACHING PRACTICE | DEFINITION | WHAT IS THE INTENT OF THE TEACHING PRACTICE? (WHY IS THIS PRACTICE PUT INTO ACTION?) |
|---|---|---|
| Ability Grouping | Students deemed to be of the same mathematics ability are grouped into a class and taught separately from other students. | |
| Within-Class Grouping | Organizing students into small groups by skill, ability, or other factors within their regular classroom. | |

Perhaps you've heard thinking like this: "We place learners in levels by math achievement (tracking) or in groups by ability (ability grouping) so that we can adjust mathematical content, pace, and instructional strategies. We want to make teaching and learning easier by placing students with similar mathematical achievement scores, levels of mathematical engagement, and math ability in the same classes." Or you may have heard: "I put my kids in math groups based on their ability. Then during mathematics, the small groups rotate every 20 minutes so that I can spend dedicated time meeting with each math group and teaching them what they're ready for." This is the intent.

But the impact of these practices does not align with the intent.

| TEACHING PRACTICE | IMPACT (EFFECT SIZE) |
|---|---|
| Tracking | 0.09 |
| Ability Grouping | 0.21 |
| Within-Class Grouping | 0.16 |

Grouping learners by mathematical ability does not improve their mathematics learning, and it does not improve our mathematics teaching. These practices communicate to learners and educators that certain people can or can't do mathematics and that nothing will change that. In fact, when learners perceive their mathematical ability is based on stereotypes about a group to which they may belong (gender, race, heritage language, special education services), this stereotype threat (ES = –0.19) has a negative impact on their mathematical learning. These practices also create inequitable access and lack of opportunity to engage in the highest levels of mathematics learning. In other words, learners from historically marginalized groups (based on race, socioeconomic status, and special education services) are placed in lower tracks and do not have access to more rigorous mathematics learning nor do they have the opportunity to grow and excel at complex mathematics concepts and skills. When we narrow and restrict *who* can do mathematics, we remove the learner from the equation and create inequity in mathematical learning and engagement.

Mathematical ability is not determined by achievement scores, interest, engagement, language, or special education services. Every person has mathematical abilities from their lived experiences, and every learner has powerful connections, nonlinguistic representations, and prior knowledge to leverage. We must communicate to every learner our high expectations, our belief that each and every one of them is capable of great mathematical thinking and learning. And then, we must follow through with that belief through our actions. When we narrow and restrict *what* mathematics is, we remove the real mathematics from the equation and create inaccuracies in mathematical learning and engagement. When we narrow and restrict *how* mathematics and mathematical learning work, we remove the meaningful connections from the equation and create incoherence in mathematical learning and engagement.

Let's return to our intentions. In this Playbook, we intend to ensure *all* learners have equity of access and opportunity to the highest level of mathematics learning possible. To align our intention and our impact, we need to value both the learners and the educators in the equation. We need to know our learners. We need to develop and leverage the expertise of ourselves—the teachers. Teaching and learning are hard work, but some instructional strategies can make teaching and learning more efficient and effective.

In this Playbook, we examine and take action to implement these instructional strategies, in which our intent and our impact align, we reframe and broaden "what it means to learn mathematics," and we pursue missed opportunities to engage *all* learners by broadening the pathways for learners to engage, represent, and demonstrate rigorous mathematics learning.

Let's begin with three instructional strategies that provide alternatives to tracking, ability grouping, and within-class grouping: differentiation, acceleration, and vocabulary instruction.

Consider why you have put these practices into action or what you've heard from others as they explain their decision-making process. You might also rely on the definition to determine the intent of the teaching practice.

| TEACHING PRACTICE | DEFINITION | WHAT IS THE INTENT OF THE TEACHING PRACTICE? (WHY IS THIS PRACTICE PUT INTO ACTION?) | IMPACT (EFFECT SIZE) |
|---|---|---|---|
| Differentiation | A wide variety of teaching techniques and lesson adaptations to meet the individual needs of a diverse group of students, including tiered tasks, recognition of multiple pathways for process and product, and varying scaffolds. | | 0.51 |
| Acceleration | Increasing the speed, decreasing the speed, or changing the direction of instruction based on learners' needs and strengths. | | 0.53 |
| Vocabulary Instruction | Building learners' specialized mathematics language (vocabulary, function, and structure), notation, and communication. | | 0.62 |

We want to highlight some unique and powerful aspects of these three instructional strategies that you may have noted in your reflection about their intentions. Differentiation has the intent of aligning individual learner's needs or next steps for learning with their individualized "just right" task and "just right" accommodation or support. Most importantly, differentiation does this *without* barring access and opportunity to the highest level of mathematics learning possible because all learners are working toward the same high expectations (learning intentions and success criteria). In other words, differentiation is not about altering the expectations or outcomes for students but about the path they take to get there and the support provided along the way. Differentiation requires taking that broadened perspective, where *all* learners are expected to engage, represent, and demonstrate rigorous mathematics learning in multiple ways.

Acceleration is not just about increasing speed, but it can also mean decreasing the speed and changing the direction of instruction. Acceleration is responsive to learners' needs and strengths in the moment based on monitoring of learners' progress toward shared high expectations (learning intentions and success criteria). Rather than relying on remediation, acceleration recognizes that all learners need some form of acceleration across the span of their learning and that individual learners need to speed up, slow down, or take a turn at different times and for different reasons.

Because mathematics is a human endeavor, the language and notation used to communicate about mathematics reflects the people using it. Therefore, the statement "Math is a universal language" is a myth. Mathematics includes highly specialized vocabulary, unique phrasings, and defined notations necessary to communicate effectively and efficiently in mathematics. The vocabulary, structure, function, and notation vary from country to country, content strand to content strand, and informal to formal settings. We cannot assume mathematics language and notation are universally and automatically understood by all. To ensure every learner has access and opportunity to the highest level of mathematics learning possible, every learner needs vocabulary instruction in mathematics. Every learner needs to meaningfully connect informal and often nonverbal mathematical knowledge with the language of mathematics.

These three instructional practices are just a beginning as we shift from awareness to action. Every module in this Playbook dives deeply into instructional strategies that ensure *all* learners have equity of access and opportunity to the highest level of mathematics learning possible.

The chart that follows contains a list of some instructional strategies that keep the pathway of mathematical learning broad and the learner at the center of our decision-making processes. As you review and reflect on the intent of each teaching practice, you might also reflect on where you are in making sense of each practice and implementing each effectively. This self-reflection may help you identify what you already do well and where you want to go next.

*(Continued)*

| TEACHING PRACTICE | DEFINITION | WHAT IS THE INTENT OF THE TEACHING PRACTICE? (WHY IS THIS PRACTICE PUT INTO ACTION?) | IMPACT (EFFECT SIZE) | MODULE OF THIS PLAYBOOK |
|---|---|---|---|---|
| Problem-Solving Teaching | Learning strategies to solve novel and rigorous problems. | | 0.61 | 7 |
| Classroom Discussion | Students discuss with each other, often prompted from an open set of questions, providing all students the opportunity to speak and learn from each other. | | 0.82 | 8 |
| Worked Examples | A task that has been completed to illustrate decision points and focus the learning on making sense of discrete problem-solving tasks within a larger complex problem. | | 0.47 | 9 |
| Scaffolding | A teacher establishes and then gradually removes outside assistance that enables students to complete mathematics tasks. | | 0.52 | 10 |
| Deliberate Practice | Challenging, effortful repetition, often adjusted through feedback that is purposeful and systematic, aimed at moving toward a particular goal. | | 0.49 | 11 |

| TEACHING PRACTICE | DEFINITION | WHAT IS THE INTENT OF THE TEACHING PRACTICE? (WHY IS THIS PRACTICE PUT INTO ACTION?) | IMPACT (EFFECT SIZE) | MODULE OF THIS PLAYBOOK |
| --- | --- | --- | --- | --- |
| Formative Evaluation | Generating evidence of and for learning in order to provide instruction and feedback during the lesson and to determine the effectiveness of the teaching strategies used. | | 0.40 | 12 |
| Co-Evaluation | Collaborating with learners to interpret evidence of learning. | | 0.75 | 13 |
| Feedback | Information provided to the learner to help close the gap between what is understood, what is aimed to be understood, and where to move next in their learning. | | 0.51 | 14 |
| Self-Regulation | Developing learners' motivation, cognition, and metacognition to drive their own learning. | | 0.51 | 15 |

# MATHEMATICAL TRUTHS

When we narrow and restrict *what* mathematics is, we remove the real mathematics from the equation and create inaccuracies in mathematical learning and engagement. In Module #4, we reflected on ways our intent can be misaligned with our impact because we are not fully embracing what it means to learn and do mathematics. As a result, we teach from and reinforce misconceptions about mathematical learning and engagement. When we narrow and restrict *how* mathematics and mathematical learning work, we remove the meaningful connections from the equation and create incoherence in mathematical learning and engagement.

Read the list of statements that follows. Circle, star, or highlight the statements that are true for you:

- Without a degree in mathematics, I don't have the expertise or knowledge to teach complex mathematics content, and so I avoid those concepts and skills.

- I need to cover as much mathematics as possible because mathematics is a vast subject with many discrete topics and skills.

- When in doubt, I teach mathematics the way I was taught mathematics.

- It's not developmentally appropriate for the youngest learners in early childhood (birth through age 8) to dive into complex mathematics concepts.

- By the end of elementary school, learners shouldn't need manipulatives anymore and should just focus on abstract reasoning.

- I teach everything through direct instruction.

- I teach everything through problem-based learning and inquiry.

These statements represent the intersection of our subject matter knowledge (knowledge of mathematics) and our pedagogical content knowledge (knowledge of how to teach mathematics). Each of us has said these statements at one time in our teaching careers. And we have certainly heard them from many teachers. But you know what's most interesting about these statements? None of them are true.

Making decisions from these false statements can lead to misalignment, missed opportunities, and misconceptions. For example, if I'm unsure of how negative numbers work or I believe negative numbers are too complex for first and second graders, I might teach the misconception that you can't subtract a larger number from a smaller number, and as a result, I also miss the opportunity to leverage learners' prior knowledge about negative temperatures, yardage, game scores, and more. If I never had the opportunity to use algebra tiles as a learner and I believe manipulatives are only for young learners, then my purely abstract teaching about variables and integers may be misaligned with what my learners are ready to make sense of, and as a result, I also miss the opportunity to engage *every* learner in making sense of systems of equations.

Read the false statements in the left column of the following table. In the middle column, make a list of misalignments, missed opportunities, and misconceptions about teaching and learning that arise from the false statements. Finally, read the true statements in the right column. These statements reflect what we know about mathematical teaching, learning, and engagement.

| FALSE STATEMENT | MISALIGNMENT, MISSED OPPORTUNITY, OR MISCONCEPTION | TRUE STATEMENT |
|---|---|---|
| Without a degree in mathematics, I don't have the expertise or knowledge to teach complex mathematics content and so I avoid those concepts and skills. | | Even without a degree in mathematics, I can intentionally develop the expertise or knowledge to teach complex mathematics content and I can begin simply by being a learner with my students. |
| I need to cover as much mathematics as possible because mathematics is a vast subject with many discrete topics and skills. | | Mathematics is an organized system of interrelated topics and skills built on relational understanding so I can focus on teaching deeply and activating learners' background knowledge so they can transfer their learning to new topics and skills. |
| When in doubt, I teach mathematics the way I was taught mathematics. | | When in doubt, I make sure I have clarity about what we're learning, why, and how we'll know we've learned it and then I plan and communicate that clarity. |
| It's not developmentally appropriate for the youngest learners in early childhood (birth through age 8) to dive into complex mathematics concepts. | | Our youngest learners in early childhood (birth through age 8) are already ready to dive into complex mathematics concepts (like probability, inverse and co-variation, patterns, equality, and comparison), in fact, they do so naturally as they explore and make sense of the world. |

*(Continued)*

(Continued)

| FALSE STATEMENT | MISALIGNMENT, MISSED OPPORTUNITY, OR MISCONCEPTION | TRUE STATEMENT |
|---|---|---|
| By the end of elementary school, learners shouldn't need manipulatives anymore and should just focus on abstract reasoning. | | Every learner at every age and within every complex concept and skill should make connections among concrete, pictorial, and abstract representations (also known as the CRA method) *and* there are manipulatives and materials to make every complex concept and skill concrete. |
| I teach everything through direct instruction. | | I teach through direct instruction when my learners are ready to learn factual information and vocabulary and to begin basic applications of that information. |
| I teach everything through problem-based learning and inquiry. | | I teach through problem-based learning and inquiry when my learners are ready to make deep connections and transfer their learning to novel situations. |

We now have a sense of where we are and what we know. We have awareness about our misalignments, missed opportunities, and misconceptions. So where do we go next? How do we shift from awareness to action?

We intentionally grow our collective teacher efficacy. In this Playbook, we hope you are collaborating with a team of educators or at least bringing your work from this Playbook to your collaborative conversations and planning sessions. Collective teacher efficacy means that *we* believe *we* can have a positive impact on students' learning and *we* can take action to do so. We shift from awareness and belief to action and evaluating impact. Look back at your reflection on pp. 97–99, and as a team, decide where to go next. Each module in Parts 3 and 4 will arm you with strategies to reframe, respond to, and revolutionize the critical challenges of learning and engagement in mathematics.

# Exit Ticket

Take a moment and self-evaluate your learning in this module using these statements.

1. I can identify and revolutionize mathematical teaching practices when the intent is misaligned with the impact.

| 1 | 2 | 3 | 4 | 5 |
|---|---|---|---|---|
| Strongly disagree | Disagree | Neutral | Agree | Strongly agree |

Explain the reason for your selection.

_____

_____

2. I can examine and pursue the missed opportunities for mathematical learning and engagement when we narrow and restrict who can do mathematics, what mathematics is, and how mathematics and mathematics learning work.

| 1 | 2 | 3 | 4 | 5 |
|---|---|---|---|---|
| Strongly disagree | Disagree | Neutral | Agree | Strongly agree |

Explain the reason for your selection.

_____

_____

3. I can explain and reframe the misconceptions about mathematical learning and engagement that impact my decision-making and teaching practices and, therefore, impact my students' learning.

| 1 | 2 | 3 | 4 | 5 |
|---|---|---|---|---|
| Strongly disagree | Disagree | Neutral | Agree | Strongly agree |

Explain the reason for your selection.

_____

_____

# What Are the Characteristics of a Rigorous Mathematics Task?

Congratulations, we have moved into Part 3 of this Playbook, which allows us to focus our attention on the design and implementation of rigorous learning tasks in our mathematics classrooms. Let's take a moment and flip back to p. 6 to remind ourselves of Big Idea #3. Fill in the blanks of our third big idea below in the box below.

---

**BIG IDEA #3**

Mathematics teaching and learning must be reflected in _____,

_____, _____, and _____ .

---

Do you recall your initial response or impression of this big idea when we first encountered the statement on p. 6? If you're like us, the term "rigor" can evoke a negative response. Rigor is a "loaded" term. Conversations in the faculty lounge, during our professional learning community (PLC+) meetings, and in the hallways of our schools often veer into the challenging topic of rigor. Phrases like "our math classes must be rigorous" or "is that assignment/task/test rigorous enough" are tossed out into the mathematics teaching and learning atmosphere with the assumption we are all talking about the same thing. Is that a safe assumption? That is the focus of this module—just as we unpacked the standards in earlier modules, we need to unpack this idea of rigorous mathematics teaching and learning.

# MODULE #7

**Learning Intention**

We are learning about rigor in mathematics teaching and learning so that we can create rigorous learning experiences across all elements of mathematics understanding.

**Success Criteria**

We'll know we've learned this when we can:

1.  describe what is meant by rigor in the mathematics classroom;

2.  evaluate our thinking regarding common misconceptions about rigorous learning;

3.  identify the relationship between rigor and strategic competence, adaptive reasoning, and productive dispositions; and

4.  describe the characteristics of an engaging task.

Take a moment and craft your own definition of rigor—when you use this term in reference to your mathematics classroom or your mathematics teaching, what specifically do you mean?

What do you mean when you say "rigor"?

_____

_____

_____

_____

As we step into our discussion of rigor, let's pull out a few key points we hope to make in this module:

1.  To ensure all learners have equity of access and opportunity to the highest level of mathematics learning possible, our mathematics tasks must be rigorous.

2.  We can adjust any task in our mathematics classrooms so that all learners have equity of access to the highest level of complex thinking possible and opportunity to be successful.

3. Some essential characteristics of a rigorous task can inform our design and implementation of those tasks across all components of mathematics teaching and learning.

Let's start with that first key point.

High-quality, high-impact mathematics teaching and learning makes good use of the time that learners are engaged with rigorous learning experiences and tasks (see Berliner, 1987, 1990). This idea is not new. The "engaged with" part of that statement is where we want to direct our attention for the next few moments. Our learners can be engaged in a learning experience or task and rigor is nowhere to be found. If you will excuse the mathematics humor, rigor is not in the solution set! On the other hand, learners can have access to a rigorous learning experience or task and not be engaged at all. Another chance for mathematics humor: The rigor yields a null result. Our desire to increase the rigor of learning in our classrooms is prompted by our learning standards and our renewed focus on a profile of a graduate or college and career readiness initiatives.

---

Take a moment and return to your work on "good" mathematics learners. On p. 67 in Module #4, you were asked to complete the sentence, "A mathematician is/can. . . ." Bring that information to this module. Either record your previous response here or revise your response based on our new learning over the past several modules.

_____

_____

_____

_____

We will come back to this list soon. Our learning experiences and tasks must, *absolutely must*, build our learners' capacity in the items you have listed here.

---

If we were to ask every one of our colleagues what rigor was and what it looked like in their future or current classrooms, we would likely get as many different responses as the number of colleagues we asked.

When the topic of rigor comes up among Mr. Rodriguez and his colleagues, "the focus immediately jumps to making it hard. I can't help but equate rigor with difficulty. I struggle with this because making something hard does not necessarily make it rigorous or lead to better learning. For example, it can be hard for an eight-year-old to sit still for 30 minutes and work on a difficult problem set. But does that mean sitting still is rigorous."

Ms. Cauley agrees. "The word hard comes to mind when rigor is discussed in our planning block. I could have them complete daily mathematics reviews in their mathematics notebooks each night at home, but to what end? I could also ask them to use vocabulary or perform tasks during math block that are clearly out of their zone of proximal development."

Ms. Napier jumps in with, "not to mention that we often are more comfortable pushing certain learners. Even if we do it inadvertently, there are some learners we challenge because we think they can do it. There are others we don't push when it comes to specific learning. But I believe they are both engaged in rigorous learning, right?"

Does this internal struggle sound familiar? Let's finally pull together our work in this module and zero in on a description of rigor in mathematics. Blackburn (2018) defined rigor as "creating an environment in which each student is expected to learn at high levels, each student is supported so he or she can learn at high levels, and each student demonstrates learning at high levels" (p. 13).

> Take a moment and reflect on this definition. Does this definition work for you? Does it eliminate the ambiguity you have about rigor? How would you combine your thoughts on p. 106 of this module with Barbara Blackburn's (2018) definition?
>
> _____
>
> _____
>
> _____
>
> _____

Before we take one more step forward in this module, return to Blackburn's (2018) definition and circle, highlight, or underline where it states that each student is supported so they can learn at high levels. The focus of this module is on rigor. The next module focuses on the ways in which we can support learners in rigorous experiences and tasks.

What this definition highlights is that we play a vital role in ensuring our learning environment is rigorous. And that is the point we are trying to make here. We must engage in the intentional, deliberate, and purposeful planning for rigorous learning experiences and tasks in our mathematics classrooms. In addition, this definition does not speak to any quantity, a specific population of learners, or test scores or grades. So, as we try to reduce the ambiguity in the term "rigor," we must also look at misconceptions associated with the term.

Much like Mr. Rodriguez, Ms. Cauley, and Ms. Napier, we all carry misconceptions about this term (see Table 7.1). Consider the following statements. Which of these do you believe are true, and which of these do you believe are false? We'll look at the "correct" answers next.

| | |
|---|---|
| 1. Lots of homework is an indicator of rigor in my mathematics classroom. | True or False |
| 2. Including more content in our mathematics classroom is rigorous. | True or False |
| 3. Not all of my learners can handle rigorous mathematics experiences and tasks. | True or False |
| 4. Scaffolding reduces the rigor in my mathematics classroom. | True or False |
| 5. The instructional materials provided to me provides the necessary rigor. | True or False |
| 6. My standards create rigor in my mathematics teaching. | True or False |
| 7. Rigor in mathematics is just a fad and will go away soon. | True or False |

TABLE 7.1 ● Misconceptions about rigor.

| MISCONCEPTION | EXPLANATION |
|---|---|
| *Lots of homework is an indicator of rigor in my mathematics classroom.* | Often, we falsely believe that providing an abundance of "things" for learners to do at home with their parents, guardians, or caregivers is promoting rigor. **This misconception is a potentially harmful belief**. Instead, this approach to rigor promotes inequity for learners that do not have access to necessary resources outside of school. Plus, learners may incorrectly practice or complete the homework. We are then required to devote a lot of time to unlearning and relearning in our classrooms.

By the way, this also applies to summer work. If your mathematics class requires summer work, you may have drifted into the second misconception. |
| *Including more content in our mathematics classroom is rigorous.* | **This misconception is also a false statement**. The coverage of more topics, tasks, and/or activities does not represent rigor. This misconception sometimes leads to expecting learners to engage with content, skills, and knowledge that are not developmentally appropriate. Learning takes time and has a strong developmental component. This may create gaps in learner's knowledge, skills, and understandings that cause problems later in their learning trajectory.

Often we attribute this misconception to the standards. That is not always true either. Allocating learning time to content, skills, and understandings that are not in the standards creates an allusion of more content. Modules #1 to #3 of this Playbook can help address this misconception. |

*(Continued)*

(Continued)

| MISCONCEPTION | EXPLANATION |
|---|---|
| *Not all of my learners can handle rigorous mathematics experiences and tasks.* | Rigorous learning experiences are often set aside for those learners that show a proclivity for mathematics. Or we only provide rigorous learning experiences and tasks in upper level courses. **This misconception is a very damaging belief.** Statements like "my students can't do that" exemplify this misconception. They reflect deficit thinking and deny some learners the access and opportunity to the highest level of complexity possible. There is a significant body of research on teacher expectations and teacher beliefs about learners. Made famous by psychologists Robert Rosenthal and Lenore Jacobson (1968), the Pygmalion Effect is a psychological phenomenon in which high expectations lead to improved performance in a given area and low expectations lead to worse (Rosenthal & Jacobson, 1992). |
| *Scaffolding reduces the rigor in my mathematics classroom.* | **This misconception is very limiting and likely occurs in tandem with other misconceptions.** The experience or task does not have to be completed independently and without any help to be rigorous. This misconception perpetuates the internal belief of learners that, "I should not ask for help." Scaffolding and support are essential components of all learners, for all learners. <br><br> This misconception often goes hand in hand with the previous belief that only certain learners can handle rigor. Scaffolding offers learners the access and opportunity to the highest level of mathematics learning possible. Take a moment and flip back to p. 108. Look at the phrase we asked you to circle, highlight, or underline. Rewrite that phrase here: <br><br> _____ . <br><br> As we mentioned, we will direct all our attention to this idea in the next module. |
| *The instructional materials provided to me provides the necessary rigor.* | There are two responses to this particular statement. First, if this were true, there would be no need for Modules #1 to #3 of this Playbook. However, that is not enough to address this **false and misleading statement**. <br><br> We often assume that the resources we are provided take rigor into account. After all, if our school district commits to a particular curriculum or program, we would assume it aligns with the expectations of rigor. Although this is not an unfair expectation, it **is a misconception**. <br><br> We must analyze the expectations, experiences, and tasks within our curricula and programs to make the necessary adaptations for the local context of our classrooms. Furthermore, how the instructional materials come to life must reflect our beliefs about "a good mathematics learner." Revisit p. 75 of this module. Finding the right level of rigor must incorporate the characteristics we strive to build in our learners. <br><br> Curricular writers and program developers do not know our students as well as we do. They cannot be held responsible for finding the right level of rigor. |

| MISCONCEPTION | EXPLANATION |
|---|---|
| *My standards create rigor in my mathematics teaching.* | **False.** Standards tell us what to teach, not how to teach it. Rigor is about the "how" and should be informed by the "who." The "who" in this case are our learners. Simply put, standards do not create rigor; they create expectations for learning. Rigor comes in how we analyze, map, and implement daily learning experiences and tasks from those standards. |
| | Rigor comes from the learning experiences and tasks that promote relational understanding, extend strategic competence, enhance adaptive reasoning, and elevate productive dispositions. |
| | Rigor is the environment in which standards come to life. This is the focus of these first seven modules and will remain the focus of the remaining eight modules. |
| *Rigor in mathematics is just a fad and will go away soon.* | **False, we hope.** If you have been around mathematics teaching and learning for longer than a millisecond, you know that things can and do change. You have likely stated or heard adults make the statement "we did not learn math that way when I was in school." They are correct, and this is a good thing. As we have learned more and more from research on mathematics teaching and learning, we have adapted our approach to the teaching and learning in our classrooms. This is how we have arrived at this moment in history. |
| | Beyond that historical viewpoint, the idea of providing learners with daily experiences that maximize their growth and development should never be considered a fad. This is what we do as teachers. This is the ethical and moral hinge point for mathematics teaching and learning. We must model strategic competence, adaptive reasoning, and productive dispositions as we learn more about what works best in teaching and learning mathematics. Do we want to have an impact or not? If not, find something else to do. |

**Source:** Adapted from Blackburn (2018).

Take a moment and process these false statements—misconceptions about rigor. Are there some we have missed? What other misconceptions have you noticed or that you have regarding the idea of rigor? Jot those down here.

_____

_____

_____

_____

*(Continued)*

(Continued)

Do you see yourself in any of these statements? If so, how will you integrate this new learning into "where to next" in your mathematics teaching? Use this space to write down your thinking.

_____

_____

_____

_____

How do each of these misconceptions directly contradict your view of what it means to be a good learner in mathematics? Revisit your notes on p. 75 or review Module #4 if necessary. Share your thinking here.

_____

_____

_____

_____

What efforts can be taken to address these misconceptions in us and in our colleagues?

_____

_____

_____

_____

The National Council of Teachers of Mathematics (NCTM, 2014) released a position statement regarding the creation, support, and sustainment of a culture of access and equity in the teaching and learning of mathematics.

Creating, supporting, and sustaining a culture of access and equity requires being responsive to students' backgrounds, experiences, cultural perspectives, traditions, and knowledge when designing and implementing a mathematics program and assessing its effectiveness. Acknowledging and addressing factors that contribute to differential outcomes among groups of students is critical to ensuring that all students routinely have opportunities to experience high-quality mathematics instruction, learn challenging mathematics content, and receive the support necessary to be successful. Addressing equity and access includes both ensuring that all students attain mathematics proficiency and increasing the numbers of students from all racial, ethnic, linguistic, gender, and socioeconomic groups who attain the highest levels of mathematics achievement (NCTM, 2014).

The misconceptions about rigor in Table 7.1 directly contradict this position statement. Yet, we should see this position statement as a belief that drives our mathematics teaching.

1. If we believe that all learners should and will be actively engaged in our mathematics learning environment, then all learners should and will be actively engaged in rigorous mathematics experiences and tasks.

2. If we believe all learners should be embraced as important members of the community, then we will offer access and opportunity to all learners to engage in rigorous tasks.

3. If we believe learners should be provided the necessary support to have an equal opportunity for success, then we will make the necessary adaptions to tasks so that all learners can engage in the highest level of rigor possible.

Rigorous standards, rigorous learning, rigorous tasks: These are common phrases in our schools and classrooms. The term "rigor" is too ambiguous to be helpful for our work with fostering, nurturing, and sustaining good mathematics learners. This ambiguity is also not helpful in building conceptual knowledge, procedural fluency, strategic competence, adaptive reasoning, and productive dispositions. If we do not take the time to address this ambiguity and nail down the domain and range of rigor, we leave the idea of rigorous mathematics teaching and learning to chance, which can create undesirable outcomes for our learners across all elements of mathematics teaching and learning.

Consider the following if–then statements related to rigor. Using our previous work on the different elements of mathematics, complete the following statements (see p. 20 in Module #1). We will provide an example to get you started. See if you can come up with a statement for each of the five elements of mathematics teaching and learning.

Too rigorous:

- Conceptual Knowledge: If rigor > learner's readiness, then <u>learners may forfeit **conceptual knowledge** and resort to memorizing facts and repeating algorithms</u>.

- Procedural Fluency: If rigor > learner's readiness, then … _____

  _____

- Strategic Competence: If rigor > learner's readiness, then … _____

  _____

*(Continued)*

(Continued)

- Adaptive Reasoning: If rigor > learner's readiness, then . . . _____

  _____

- Productive Dispositions: If rigor > learner's readiness then . . . _____

  _____

Not rigorous enough:

- Conceptual Knowledge: If rigor < learner's readiness, <u>then learners will not stretch their thinking and not develop or use adaptive reasoning.</u>

- Procedural Fluency: If rigor < learner's readiness, then . . . _____

  _____

- Strategic Competence: If rigor < learner's readiness, then . . . _____

  _____

- Adaptive Reasoning: If rigor < learner's readiness, then . . . _____

  _____

- Productive Dispositions: If rigor < learner's readiness then . . . _____

  _____

You likely noticed that these if–then statements highlight the interconnectedness of the elements of mathematics teaching and learning. Too much rigor may shift learners' attention to simply memorizing facts and repeating algorithms. Too little rigor removes the impetus to engage in adaptive reasoning. The message here is that rigor is relevant in mathematics teaching and learning.

Rigor is for everyone, not just a selected few. Rigor is about moving learning forward. Therefore, we must intentionally, deliberately, and purposefully design learning experiences and tasks to include elements that enhance the quality for all learners based on what they need to move their learning forward. This process includes but is not limited to:

- access to complex problems and authentic scenarios that require strategic competence, adaptive reasoning, and productive dispositions;

- a focus on extracting and leveraging conceptual knowledge to explain thinking;

- the opportunity to build background knowledge through Math Talk;

- a balance between conceptual knowledge and procedural fluency; and

- integrating mathematics into other content areas.

Before we close out this module, we want to lay additional foundation for the next several modules. In addition to how we scaffold learning experiences and tasks so that all learners can experience the right level of rigor, we need to lay down what the research says about engaging mathematical experiences and tasks. We asserted that learners can have access to a rigorous learning experience or task and not be engaged at all. So, what are the non-negotiables in an engaging mathematics experience or task?

Before we sort through the research, take a moment and think of a mathematics experience or task that really engaged your learners. Jot down the characteristics or essential features of that engaging experience or task.

_____

_____

Then, think of a mathematics experience or task that did not engage your learners. Jot down the characteristics or features of that experience or task.

_____

_____

Now compare and contrast the two. How were they similar? How were they different?

_____

_____

_____

_____

## ESSENTIAL CHARACTERISTICS OF AN ENGAGING MATHEMATICS EXPERIENCE OR TASK

What separates an engaging task from one that learners are simply not motivated or interested in tackling is the nature of the engagement required to participate in the experience or complete the task. Learners typically fail to see the value in tasks that ask them to simply repeat algorithms, select and execute procedures, and solve inauthentic or irrelevant problems. In other words, finding the right level of rigor must begin with finding the right level of engagement, not boredom. Antonetti and Garver (2015) reported on data from more than 17,000 classroom walkthroughs and identified eight features of classroom tasks that differentiated those tasks that fostered, nurtured, and sustained student engagement from those that did not capture learners. Let's look at these eight characteristics and use them as a checks-and-balance system for our own mathematics experiences and tasks.

*Clear and Modeled Expectations.* Do learners have a clear understanding of what they are supposed to know, understand, and be able to do? This characteristic refers us back to clear learning intentions, success criteria, learning progressions, exemplars, models, and examples. Do your learners know what success looks like, or are they blindly hoping to hit the end target that you have in mind for them? We devoted significant time to this idea in Modules #1 through #3.

How do you communicate clear and modeled expectations in your mathematics classroom? Give some specific examples.

_____

_____

_____

_____

*Emotional Safety.* Do learners feel safe in asking questions, making mistakes, or trying things out in the task? To be blunt, if learners feel threatened in our classrooms, they will not engage in any task. Preservation of self takes precedence over the completion of a task. This often shows up as disruptive behavior or apathy. If we truly have a productive learning environment, this particular feature of our tasks is present every time. We will turn our attention toward this concept later in the Playbook.

How do you promote emotional safety in your mathematics classroom? Give some specific examples.

_____

_____

_____

_____

*Personal Response.* Do learners have the opportunity to bring their personal experiences to the learning experience? Examples include any strategy or learning experience that invites learners to bring their backgrounds, interests, or expertise to the conversation. This might be an activity that provides learners with the option to create their own analogies or metaphors, allowing learners to select how they will share their responses to a question (e.g., writing, drawing, speaking), or letting learners select the context in which a concept is explored (e.g., allowing learners to select a specific book or create their own problems). These examples have one thing in common: They allow learners to personalize their responses to meet their backgrounds, interests, or expertise.

How do you make room for personal response in your mathematics classroom? Give some specific examples.

_____

_____

_____

_____

*Sense of Audience.* Do learners have a sense that this work matters to someone other than the teacher and the grade book? Tasks that provide learners a sense of audience are those tasks that mean something to individuals beyond the teacher, and these tasks provide authenticity. Sense of audience can be established by collaborative learning or group work where individual members have specific roles, as in a jigsaw activity. Other examples include community-based projects or service projects that contribute to the local, school, or classroom community. We will take a closer look at this in the next several modules.

How do you create a sense of audience in your mathematics classroom? Give some specific examples.

_____

_____

_____

_____

*Social Interaction.* Do learners have opportunities to socially interact with their peers? How about us? Providing learners with opportunities to talk about their learning and interact with their peers supports their meaning-making and development of conceptual knowledge, adaptive reasoning, strategic competence, and productive dispositions. In addition, teachers and learners get to hear other students' ideas. Learning is social, and a quiet classroom stifles the social aspect of teaching and learning. Our tasks should provide multiple opportunities for learners to talk out ideas and exchange those ideas with peers. Academic discourse improves language skills and communications skills, along with understanding. This is the exact topic of Module #8.

> What role does social interaction play in your mathematics classroom? Give some specific examples.
>
> _____
>
> _____
>
> _____
>
> _____

*Choice.* Do learners have choices in how they access the learning? As learners engage with conceptual knowledge, mathematical processes, and essential understandings, we should offer choices around who they work with, what materials and manipulatives are available, and what problem-solving approaches learners can use to move their thinking forward. In addition, we should offer them multiple ways to show us their relational understanding.

> How do you offer choice in your mathematics classroom? Give some specific examples.
>
> _____
>
> _____
>
> _____
>
> _____

*Novelty.* Do learners experience the learning from a new or unique perspective? How can we present content in a way that captures their attention? How do we use a similar approach to provide learners with perspectives that are different from their own? Having learners assume roles is one way to approach this particular characteristic of an engaging task. Getting the chance to be an actuary, a pharmacist, a civil engineer, an operating room nurse, a professional baker, or a chemist can go a long way in fostering, nurturing, and sustaining engagement.

How do you leverage novelty in your mathematics classroom? Give some specific examples.

_____

_____

_____

_____

*Authenticity.* Finally, do learners experience an authentic learning experience, or is the experience sterile and unrealistic (e.g., a worksheet versus a problem-solving scenario)? Authenticity simply means that the task reflects something that could or does happen in the world outside of the classroom. For example, creating a class garden that requires you to maximize the area and perimeter with limited resources or gathering, analyzing, and representing data from a school survey.

How do you provide authentic experiences and tasks in your mathematics classroom? Give some specific examples.

_____

_____

_____

_____

Rigor is a necessary and sufficient condition for fostering, nurturing, and sustaining mathematics learning. Rigor helps us approach the teaching and learning of mathematics in a way that ensures all learners have equity of access and opportunity to the highest level of mathematics learning possible. However, rigor first requires an engaging experience or task that invites learners to step into and accept the challenge of a rigorous task.

This module has laid the foundation for the subsequent modules around designing and implementing rigorous mathematical experiences and tasks. Now we turn our attention to "how." How do we do this? How do we move this from an idea to integrating rigor into our mathematics classroom? The "how" begins in Module #8.

## Exit Ticket

Take a moment and self-evaluate your own learning in this module using these statements.

1. I can describe what is meant by rigor in the mathematics classroom.

| 1 | 2 | 3 | 4 | 5 |
|---|---|---|---|---|
| Strongly disagree | Disagree | Neutral | Agree | Strongly agree |

Explain the reason for your selection.

_____

_____

2. I can evaluate my thinking regarding common misconceptions about rigorous learning.

| 1 | 2 | 3 | 4 | 5 |
|---|---|---|---|---|
| Strongly disagree | Disagree | Neutral | Agree | Strongly agree |

Explain the reason for your selection.

_____

_____

3. I can identify the relationship between rigor and strategic competence, adaptive reasoning, and productive dispositions.

| 1 | 2 | 3 | 4 | 5 |
|---|---|---|---|---|
| Strongly disagree | Disagree | Neutral | Agree | Strongly agree |

Explain the reason for your selection.

_____

_____

4. I can describe the characteristics of an engaging task.

| 1 | 2 | 3 | 4 | 5 |
|---|---|---|---|---|
| Strongly disagree | Disagree | Neutral | Agree | Strongly agree |

Explain the reason for your selection.

_____

_____

# MODULE 8

# How Do I Facilitate Math Talk in My Classroom?

## MODULE #8

**Learning Intention**

We are learning about Math Talk so that we can provide students with rigorous mathematical experiences and opportunities for all learners to engage in mathematical discourse.

**Success Criteria**

We'll know we've learned this when we can:

1. explain the benefits of mathematical discourse,

2. describe the components of a Math-Talk learning community, and

3. recognize opportunities to develop students' ability to communicate with the language of mathematics.

## WHY DISCOURSE MATTERS

As you may have guessed from the title, the focus of this module is *Math Talk*. However, we want to take a step back and think about the extent to which discourse plays a role in mathematical teaching and learning. Teachers are not simply the providers of knowledge; they should guide and extend students' thinking as the class listens and learns to accept other students' ideas (Ball, 1993).

Vygotsky (1976) described discourse as a platform on which students communicate their mathematical ideas with teachers and peers to share their understanding, clarify misperceptions, and evaluate ideas. The National Council of Teachers of Mathematics (NCTM, 2014) went further and stated that in discourse-rich classrooms, students work in pairs, small groups, and as a whole class to share ideas and clarify understandings, construct convincing arguments regarding why and how things work, develop a language for expressing mathematical ideas, and see things from other perspectives. Although content standards vary from state to state, members of the academic community share expectations regarding the need for students to engage in discourse.

Take a moment to find a copy of your state standards of mathematical practice (if you don't have them readily available, don't worry; we included NCTM's process standards in Figure 8.1). Highlight or circle every standard that directly involves students engaging in discourse. Then answer the follow-up questions in the space provided so that we can revisit them throughout our work in this Playbook.

How frequently do themes regarding discourse occur in your standards? What does this indicate about how often students need to engage in discourse?

_____

_____

_____

_____

**FIGURE 8.1** ● NCTM's five process standards.

**Problem Solving**

**Instructional programs from prekindergarten through grade 12 should enable each and every student to—**

- Build new mathematical knowledge through problem solving
- Solve problems that arise in mathematics and in other contexts
- Apply and adapt a variety of appropriate strategies to solve problems
- Monitor and reflect on the process of mathematical problem solving

**Reasoning and Proof**

**Instructional programs from prekindergarten through grade 12 should enable each and every student to—**

- Recognize reasoning and proof as fundamental aspects of mathematics
- Make and investigate mathematical conjectures

- Develop and evaluate mathematical arguments and proofs
- Select and use various types of reasoning and methods of proof

**Communication**

**Instructional programs from prekindergarten through grade 12 should enable each and every student to—**

- Organize and consolidate their mathematical thinking through communication
- Communicate their mathematical thinking coherently and clearly to peers, teachers, and others
- Analyze and evaluate the mathematical thinking and strategies of others
- Use the language of mathematics to express mathematical ideas precisely

**Connections**

**Instructional programs from prekindergarten through grade 12 should enable each and every student to—**

- Recognize and use connections among mathematical ideas
- Understand how mathematical ideas interconnect and build on one another to produce a coherent whole
- Recognize and apply mathematics in contexts outside of mathematics

**Representation**

**Instructional programs from prekindergarten through grade 12 should enable each and every student to—**

- Create and use representations to organize, record, and communicate mathematical ideas
- Select, apply, and translate among mathematical representations to solve problems
- Use representations to model and interpret physical, social, and mathematical phenomena

**Source:** Reprinted from Standards & Positions, in National Council of Teachers of Mathematics (n.d.). Copyright 2000 by National Council of Teachers of Mathematics. Reprinted with permission.

Henningsen and Stein (1997) noted that teachers are charged with pressing students to provide meaningful explanations to help support higher level mathematical thinking and reasoning. It is not enough for students to think like mathematicians; they need to communicate like them as well. As E. M. Forster, an English author, asked, "How do I know what I think until I see what I say?" A classroom that provides meaningful discourse offers many opportunities for speaking, reading, listening, and writing (Walter, 2018). Students must process information, share ideas, listen and respond to others, and collaborate on a consensus, which often requires clarification questions, summarization of key concepts, connection of relevant ideas, and analysis of conversations (Walter, 2018). If students cannot access and participate in discourse, their opportunities to learn mathematics may be diminished (Banse et al., 2016). How can we assess what students know or are able to do without discourse? More importantly, how can students assess their own learning if they don't use the language of mathematics to reflect and refine their thinking?

Reflect on your mathematics teaching and your students' mathematics learning. In what ways do you have students speak, listen, read, and write in the language of mathematics? Jot the various activities and tools you use to support these four areas down in the space below so that we can revisit them throughout our work in this Playbook.

In what ways do my students:

- speak like a mathematician?

_____

_____

- listen like a mathematician?

_____

_____

- read like a mathematician?

_____

_____

- write like a mathematician?

_____

_____

## UNDERSTANDING MATH TALKS

Math Talks are respectful but engaged conversations in which students can clarify their thinking and learn from others through talk (Chapin et al., 2009). They are daily, rigorous teaching and learning experiences for all students, where meaningful mathematical discussions construct knowledge and support mathematical learning of all participants (Hufferd-Ackles et al., 2004). When students engage in Math Talks, they:

- increase their mathematical knowledge and understanding because they are held responsible for justifying their reasoning (Rawding & Wills, 2012);

- have a voice and use strategies for overcoming difficulties through discussion (Gresham & Shannon, 2017);

- concentrate on reasoning and making sense of mathematics (Gresham & Shannon, 2017);

- clarify their thinking and learn from others through talk (Chapin et al., 2009);

- develop their metacognition and discuss, debate, and reevaluate situations in a respectful manner (Walter, 2019); and

- discover misunderstandings, deepen meaning, boost memory, and develop language and social skills (Chapin et al., 2009).

Before we continue, let's revisit the learning from the previous module. In Module #7, we defined "rigorous mathematics task" and identified its essential characteristics. Consider the ways in which a Math Talk is a rigorous task and justify your thinking. Jot down your reasoning in the space below so that we can revisit it throughout our work in this Playbook.

Characteristics of a Rigorous Mathematics Task

A Math Talk is a rigorous mathematics task because . . .

_____

_____

# ELEMENTS OF MATH TALKS

Hufferd-Ackles et al. (2004) studied Math-Talk learning communities and identified four distinct but interrelated components:

1) **Questioning:** This looks closely at who is the questioner in classroom interactions. Is the teacher exclusively asking questions, or do students share this role alongside the teacher?

2) **Explaining Mathematical Thinking:** Although this connects with questioning, it focuses on students' ability to fully and fluidly explain their mathematical thinking. Did they contribute in a significant way, such that the teacher and other students can assess, question, or build on their ideas?

3) **Source of Mathematical Ideas:** This component compares the teacher's level of involvement with the students. Are students expected to mimic what the teacher models, or does the teacher elicit students' ideas such that their involvement directs the learning?

4) **Responsibility for Learning:** The final component concentrates on students' role in their learning journey. Are they passive listeners, or are they engaged and involved in the classroom discourse as co-learners and co-teachers?

From their research, Hufferd-Ackles et al. (2004) developed a framework that categorizes Math Talks into four levels, Level 0 to 3 (see Figure 8.2).

**FIGURE 8.2** ● Levels of the Math-Talk Learning Community: Action Trajectories for teacher and student.

**OVERVIEW OF SHIFT OVER LEVELS 0—3: THE CLASSROOM COMMUNITY GROWS TO SUPPORT STUDENTS ACTING IN CENTRAL OR LEADING ROLES AND SHIFTS FROM A FOCUS ON ANSWERS TO A FOCUS ON MATHEMATICAL THINKING.**

| A. QUESTIONING | B. EXPLAINING MATHEMATICAL THINKING | C. SOURCE OF MATHEMATICAL IDEAS | D. RESPONSIBILITY FOR LEARNING |
|---|---|---|---|
| Shift from teacher as questioner to students and teacher as questioners. | Students increasingly explain and articulate their math ideas. | Shift from teacher as the source of all math ideas to students' ideas also influencing direction of lesson. | Students increasingly take responsibility for learning and evaluation of others and self. Math sense becomes the criterion for evaluation. |

**LEVEL 0: TRADITIONAL TEACHER-DIRECTED CLASSROOM WITH BRIEF ANSWER RESPONSES FROM STUDENTS.**

| A. QUESTIONING | B. EXPLAINING MATHEMATICAL THINKING | C. SOURCE OF MATHEMATICAL IDEAS | D. RESPONSIBILITY FOR LEARNING |
|---|---|---|---|
| *Teacher is the only questioner. Short frequent questions function to keep students listening and paying attention to the teacher.* | *No or minimal teacher elicitation of student thinking, strategies, or explanations; teacher expects answer-focused responses. Teacher may tell answers.* | *Teacher is physically at the board, usually chalk in hand, telling and showing students how to do math.* | *Teacher repeats student responses (originally directed to her) for the class. Teacher responds to students' answers by verifying the correct answer or showing the correct method.* |
| Students give short answers and respond to the teacher only. No student-to-student Math Talk. | No student thinking or strategy-focused explanation of work. Only answers are given. | Students respond to math presented by the teacher. They do not offer their own math ideas. | Students are passive listeners; they attempt to imitate the teacher and do not take responsibility for the learning of their peers or themselves. |

## LEVEL 1. TEACHER BEGINNING TO PURSUE STUDENT MATHEMATICAL THINKING. TEACHER PLAYS CENTRAL ROLE IN THE MATH-TALK COMMUNITY.

| A. QUESTIONING | B. EXPLAINING MATHEMATICAL THINKING | C. SOURCE OF MATHEMATICAL IDEAS | D. RESPONSIBILITY FOR LEARNING |
|---|---|---|---|
| Teacher questions begin to focus on student thinking and focus less on answers. Teacher begins to ask follow-up questions about student methods and answers. Teacher is still the only questioner. | Teacher probes student thinking somewhat. One or two strategies may be elicited. Teacher may fill in explanations herself. | Teacher is still the main source of ideas, though she elicits some student ideas. Teacher does some probing to access student ideas. | Teacher begins to set up structures to facilitate students listening to and helping other students. The teacher alone gives feedback. |
| As a student answers a question, other students listen passively or wait for their turn. | Students give information about their math thinking usually as it is probed by the teacher (minimal volunteering of thoughts). They provide brief descriptions of their thinking. | Some student ideas are raised in discussions, but are not explored. | Students become more engaged by repeating what other students say or by helping another student at the teacher's request. This helping mostly involves students showing how they solved a problem. |

## LEVEL 2: TEACHER MODELING AND HELPING STUDENTS BUILD NEW ROLES. SOME CO-TEACHING AND CO-LEARNING BEGINS AS STUDENT-TO-STUDENT TALK INCREASES. TEACHER PHYSICALLY BEGINS TO MOVE TO SIDE OR BACK OF THE ROOM.

| A. QUESTIONING | B. EXPLAINING MATHEMATICAL THINKING | C. SOURCE OF MATHEMATICAL IDEAS | D. RESPONSIBILITY FOR LEARNING |
|---|---|---|---|
| Teacher continues to ask probing questions and also asks more open questions. She also facilitates student-to-student talk, e.g., by asking students to be prepared to ask questions about other students' work. | Teacher probes more deeply to learn about student thinking and supports detailed descriptions from students. Teacher open to and elicits multiple strategies. | Teacher follows up on explanations and builds on them by asking students to compare and contrast them. Teacher is comfortable using student errors as opportunities for learning. | Teacher encourages student responsibility for understanding the mathematical ideas of others. Teacher asks other students questions about student work and whether they agree or disagree and why. |

(Continued)

## LEVEL 2: TEACHER MODELING AND HELPING STUDENTS BUILD NEW ROLES. SOME CO-TEACHING AND CO-LEARNING BEGINS AS STUDENT-TO-STUDENT TALK INCREASES. TEACHER PHYSICALLY BEGINS TO MOVE TO SIDE OR BACK OF THE ROOM.

| A. QUESTIONING | B. EXPLAINING MATHEMATICAL THINKING | C. SOURCE OF MATHEMATICAL IDEAS | D. RESPONSIBILITY FOR LEARNING |
|---|---|---|---|
| Students ask questions of one another's work on the board, often at the prompting of the teacher. Students listen to one another so they do not repeat questions. | Students usually give information as it is probed by the teacher with some volunteering of thoughts. They begin to stake a position and articulate more information in response to probes. They explain steps in their thinking by providing fuller descriptions and begin to defend their answers and methods. Other students listen supportively. | Students exhibit confidence about their ideas and share their own thinking and strategies even if they are different from others. Student ideas sometimes guide the direction of the math lesson. | Students begin to listen to understand one another. When the teacher requests, they explain other students' ideas in their own words. Helping involves clarifying *other students'* ideas for themselves and others. Students imitate and model teacher's probing in pair work and in whole-class discussions. |

## LEVEL 3: TEACHER AS CO-TEACHER AND CO-LEARNER. TEACHER MONITORS ALL THAT OCCURS, STILL FULLY ENGAGED. TEACHER IS READY TO ASSIST, BUT NOW IN MORE PERIPHERAL AND MONITORING ROLE (COACH AND ASSISTER).

| QUESTIONING | EXPLAINING MATHEMATICAL THINKING | SOURCE OF MATHEMATICAL IDEAS | RESPONSIBILITY FOR LEARNING |
|---|---|---|---|
| *Teacher expects students to ask one another questions about their work. The teacher's questions still may guide the discourse.* | *Teacher follows along closely to student descriptions of their thinking, encouraging students to make their explanations more compete; may ask probing questions to make explanations more complete. Teacher stimulates students to think more deeply about strategies.* | *Teacher allows for interruptions from students during her explanations; she lets students explain and "own" new strategies. (Teacher is still engaged and deciding what is important to continue exploring.) Teacher uses student ideas and methods as the basis for lessons or miniextensions.* | *The teacher expects students to be responsible for co-evaluation of everyone's work and thinking. She supports students as they help one another sort out misconceptions. She helps and/or follows up when needed.* |
| Student-to-student talk is student-initiated, not dependent on the teacher. Students ask questions and listen to responses. Many questions are "Why?" questions that require justification from the person answering. Students repeat their own or other's questions until satisfied with answers. | Students describe more complete strategies; they *defend and justify* their answers with little prompting from the teacher. Students realize that they will be asked questions from other students when they finish, so they are motivated and careful to be thorough. Other students support with active listening. | Students interject their ideas as the teacher or other students are teaching, confident that their ideas are valued. Students spontaneously compare and contrast and build on ideas. Student ideas form part of the content of many math lessons. | Students listen to understand, then initiate clarifying other students' work and ideas for themselves and for others during whole-class discussions as well as in small group and pair work. Students assist each other in understanding and correcting errors. |

**Note:** Overview of teacher and student shifts over Levels 0–3 in Math-Talk learning communities. Adapted from "Describing Levels and Components of a Math-Talk Learning Community," by Hufferd-Ackles et al. (2004), *Journal for Research in Mathematics Education, 35,* (pp. 88–90). Copyright 2004 by the National Council of Teachers of Mathematics.

Reflect on your mathematics teaching and your students' mathematics learning. Which one of the four levels best describes the Math-Talk learning community in your classroom? Jot your thoughts down in the space below so that we can revisit them throughout our work in this Playbook.

_____

_____

_____

_____

## STRATEGIES FOR EFFECTIVE MATH TALKS

A student may not enter our classrooms as an expert in mathematical discourse, but we can help them become one before they leave. Deciding which aspects of productive discourse to teach will depend on students' previous experiences with classroom discourse, students' ages, and current classroom dynamics (Water, 2018). To help us think through these decisions, Zwiers et al. (2014) suggested that teachers should be able to answer these questions:

- What do I want to see and hear?
- How can I teach students the best things to say next in conversation?
- How can I teach cohesion in taking turns and whole conversation?
- How do I teach listening?
- Which conversation skills can I teach?

Wagganer (2015) suggested the following five strategies that encourage meaningful Math Talk:

1) Discuss why Math Talk is important.
2) Teach students how to listen and respond.
3) Introduce sentence stems.
4) Contrast explanation versus justification.
5) Give an example.

When students understand why Math Talks are important, they properly engage in meaningful mathematics discussions (Wagganer, 2015). Invite students to share their reasons for why Math Talks are important and how they individually and collectively benefit from them. They will often acknowledge how working together, like in small groups, helps them to learn to work autonomously to make sense of mathematics. It also influences what gets worked on during the concluding discussion because the teacher often uses this time to monitor and guide students' thinking around key mathematical ideas and uses their observations to determine which strategies to highlight during the whole-class discussion (Smith et al., 2009).

Before we ask our students to think about their answers, let's take a moment to think about our response and anticipate theirs. Why do **you** believe Math Talks are important? How do they support our mathematical teaching and students' mathematical learning? Jot your responses down in the space below so that we can revisit them throughout our work in this Playbook.

_____

_____

_____

_____

The second strategy requires us to provide explicit instruction on listening and revoicing techniques. Listening skills can include restating, summarizing, and connecting (Gresham & Shannon, 2017). Wagganer (2015) explained that active listening involves listening to the speaker and trying to understand the complete meaning behind what is being said and listed the following five steps:

1. Pay attention to the speaker.

2. Show you are listening through verbal and nonverbal cues.

3. Provide feedback by asking questions or summarizing what the speaker is saying.

4. Allow the speaker to finish before asking questions or stating opinions.

5. Respond appropriately by being open, honest, and respectful.

The revoicing technique is when the listener repeats part or all of the speaker's words and asks the speaker to say whether the repeated words are correct (Chapin et al., 2013) using precise mathematical language (O'Connor & Michaels, 1993). This technique has a dual purpose: to share the student's response with the class while affirming or adapting the student's answer as necessary (Banse et al., 2016). McNeil (2012) identified the following three types of revoicing:

- **Repetition:** The listener repeats the speaker's response word for word.
- **Elaboration:** The listener, either the teacher or a student, will extend a speaker's response.
- **Reformulation:** Either the teacher or a student rephrases a speaker's response using precise mathematical language.

Sentence stems are tools that help students craft a response when they participate in Math Talks (Rawding & Willis, 2012). When given time to process beforehand, students talk more productively because they clarify their thinking, deepen their understanding, and engage in the reasoning of others (Chapin et al., 2009). Sentence stems support the speaking, listening, reading, and writing language modalities (see Figure 8.3). Used as writing tools, they can lead to meaningful discourse (Walter, 2018; Witzel & Little, 2016). Students who write about their reasoning develop their mathematics vocabulary, organize their thoughts, and develop problem-solving methods (Furner & Berman, 2012).

**FIGURE 8.3** ● Sentence stems.

1. I agree with _____ because . . .

2. What I think is . . .

3. I see this differently because . . .

4. I made a connection with what _____ said . . .

5. When I thought about the question, I thought back to . . .

6. I chose this method because . . .

**Note:** Adapted from "Discourse: Simple Moves That Work," by Rawding and Wills (2012), "Mathematics Teaching in the Middle School," 18, pp. 46–51. Copyright 2004 by the National Council of Teachers of Mathematics.

What other strategies or tools do you use in your practice to develop language skills? Jot your responses down in the space below so that we can revisit them throughout our work in this Playbook.

_____

_____

_____

_____

Students may need our support in understanding the distinction between explanation and justification, which is why teachers should explicitly call out who they contrast (Wagganer, 2015). Both have their place in mathematical discourse, but students need to know why and how they are different. In simple terms, we *explain* our ideas, strategies, and solutions, whereas we *justify* after we compare, contrast, or connect our ideas, strategies, and solutions. Open-ended questions are great examples to use to model mathematical teaching and practice mathematical learning through these two modes of communication. In contrast, closed or low-level questions promote little accountability to produce a response, are disconnected with the material, require little cognitive load, and negate the need for discussion between partners (Walter, 2019). Open-ended questions have responses that teachers cannot easily anticipate (McNeil, 2012) and are usually followed by an opportunity for students to explain ("how") and justify their mathematical thinking ("why"). They are another critical tool for productive discourse, essential for all students' mathematical development because they elicit mathematical reasoning from students and focus on conceptual, rather than on procedural, understanding (Banse et al., 2016).

Take a moment to find a copy of your state standards of mathematical practice (if you don't have them readily available, don't worry; we included NCTM's process standards in Figure 8.1). Highlight or circle every standard that directly involves students engaging in discourse. Then answer the follow-up questions in the space provided so that we can revisit them throughout our work in this Playbook.

How frequently do themes regarding discourse occur in your standards? What does this indicate about how often students need to engage in discourse?

_____

_____

_____

_____

We hope you agree that Math Talks is an effective, rigorous teaching and learning experience that should be implemented daily as part of our instruction. Revisit Hufferd-Ackles et al.'s (2004) four components for Math Talks. What practices will you start, stop, or continue doing to develop mathematical discourse? Jot down your thinking and apply key takeaways in the space below so that we can revisit them throughout our work in this Playbook.

| MATH TALK COMPONENTS | START | STOP | CONTINUE |
|---|---|---|---|
| 1. Questioning | | | |
| 2. Explaining mathematical thinking | | | |
| 3. Source of mathematical ideas | | | |
| 4. Responsibility for learning | | | |

# Exit Ticket

Take a moment and self-evaluate your learning in this module using these statements.

1. I can explain the benefits of mathematical discourse.

| 1 | 2 | 3 | 4 | 5 |
|---|---|---|---|---|
| Strongly disagree | Disagree | Neutral | Agree | Strongly agree |

Explain the reason for your selection.

_____

_____

2. I can describe the components of a Math-Talk learning community.

| 1 | 2 | 3 | 4 | 5 |
|---|---|---|---|---|
| Strongly disagree | Disagree | Neutral | Agree | Strongly agree |

Explain the reason for your selection.

_____

_____

3. I can recognize opportunities to develop students' ability to communicate with the language of mathematics.

| 1 | 2 | 3 | 4 | 5 |
|---|---|---|---|---|
| Strongly disagree | Disagree | Neutral | Agree | Strongly agree |

Explain the reason for your selection.

_____

_____

# How Do I Implement Worked Examples Into My Classroom?

## MODULE #9

**Learning Intention**

We are learning about worked examples so that we can use them to deepen students' procedural and conceptual knowledge and correct common misconceptions more effectively.

**Success Criteria**

We'll know we've learned this when we can:

1. identify the three types of worked examples,

2. explain the differences between each type of worked example, and

3. create our own worked examples to use in our mathematics instruction.

## ACTIVATING PRIOR KNOWLEDGE

Let's start with a warm-up before we jump into this module. In the space provided, jot down the similarities and differences between a "solving an example problem" and a "worked example problem." In what circumstances have you chosen to incorporate each one into your instruction? What are their benefits?

_____

_____

_____

_____

# UNDERSTANDING WORKED EXAMPLES

Sweller and Cooper (1985) summarized mathematical instruction into three stereotypical steps: (1) introduce students to relevant information consisting of principles and relations; (2) demonstrate the use of the new material through a small number of example problems and solutions; and (3) present students with a large number of problems to solve. They also noted that instead of dedicating so much time to problem solving, there should be heavier use of worked examples to optimize schema acquisition.

A worked example is a problem that is fully completed and is used to demonstrate a procedure (R. C. Clark et al., 2011). Worked examples direct students' attention to certain steps of the task as a focus of questioning (Lange et al., 2014). With time, students can extract mathematical principles and common features for solving a problem, avoid cognitive overload, and progress toward automation of problem solving in that domain (Barbieri et al., 2023). By no means are these principles novel to the mathematical classroom, yet making this shift toward using worked examples within the instruction is shown to positively impact students.

Researchers found that when learners identify and explain the reasoning behind the steps that they see carried out, there is a positive influence on learning in both traditional (Booth et al., 2011) and online classroom spaces (Booth et al., 2013). Students make fewer errors, complete follow-up problems faster, and require less teacher assistance (W. M. Carroll, 1994; Sweller & Cooper, 1985). This approach to mathematical teaching and learning offers a way for them to confront their misconceptions and replace them with a deeper conceptual understanding (Lange et al., 2014).

## THREE TYPES OF WORKED EXAMPLES

Three types of worked examples exist: correct, partially complete, and incorrect work examples (see Figures 9.1 and 9.2). Teachers are comfortable with implementing the first two but may be apprehensive about presenting incorrect examples for fear that they will lead to confusion. It is not enough to ask learners to simply identify the error in the incorrect example. To go beyond procedural thinking and into conceptual knowledge, we invite them to explain or justify their thinking through prompts (see Figure 9.3).

**FIGURE 9.1** ● Samples of worked examples.

| WORKED EXAMPLES | EXAMPLES |
| --- | --- |
| Correct | Sunny solved the equation correctly. Look at her work and then answer the questions below. $$\frac{3(2-4x)}{3} = \frac{-24}{3}$$ $$\begin{aligned} 2-4x &= -8 \\ -2 & \qquad -2 \\ \hline -4x &= -10 \\ \overline{-4} & \quad \overline{-4} \\ x &= 5/2 \end{aligned}$$ Would the solution be the same for the equation $6 - 12x = -24$? What about $12 - 24x = -48$? Explain why or why not. |

*(Continued)*

(Continued)

| WORKED EXAMPLES | EXAMPLES |
|---|---|
| Partially Completed | David started evaluating the algebraic expression and then he got stuck. Help him finish the rest of the problem. <br><br> $-5(x+7) - x + 4^x$ for $x = -2$ <br> $-5(-2+7) - (-2) + 4^{(-2)}$ <br> $-5(5) + 2 + 4^{-2}$ |
| Incorrect | Jeffrey tried solving the quadratic equation, but he didn't do it correctly. Where did he go wrong? What is the correct solution? <br><br> $(x-1)^2 = 17$ <br> $x^2 + 1 = 17$ <br> $\quad -1 \quad -1$ <br> $\overline{\qquad\qquad}$ <br> $x^2 = 16$ <br> $x = \pm 4$ |

Booth et al. (2015) supported the notion that students who use correct and incorrect examples had better conceptual and procedural understanding and performed better on standardized tests when compared with their peers who did not use them. Furthermore, worked examples resulted in gains in conceptual knowledge that were even greater for struggling students (Booth et al., 2015) and mitigated negative impacts of mathematics anxiety on students' procedural and conceptual understanding, situational interest in the lesson, and mind wandering during testing (Mesghin et al., 2023).

**FIGURE 9.2** ● Prompts for worked examples.

| WORKED EXAMPLES | STUDENT PROMPTS |
|---|---|
| Correct | • Explain the work shown for a particular task<br>• Extend the work to a second part<br>• Answer a question about the response<br>• Offer an alternative approach<br>• Explain how they know it is correct<br>• Determine how the correct response might have been found |
| Partially Completed | • Complete work where a student was stuck, and explain the reasoning behind the steps to complete the work<br>• Complete a student's work, and answer a question about the work |
| Incorrect | • Find the error, fix it, and explain the fix<br>• Fix the incorrect response, and complete the work<br>• Explain why an incorrect response is incorrect<br>• Explain why the item is incorrect and then complete it correctly<br>• Answer a question about the incorrect work on the item |

**Source:** Adapted from C. Carroll et al. (2016).

**FIGURE 9.3** ● Sample prompts.

| WORKED EXAMPLES | POTENTIAL STUDENT PROMPTS |
|---|---|
| Correct | • Explain the thinking behind one or all steps in your own words.<br>• Is there another way to solve this problem?<br>• Is your method similar or different than the worked example? |
| Partially Completed | • Explain why the student was stuck.<br>• How would you help them get "unstuck"?<br>• Begin where they got stuck and finish the rest of the problem. |
| Incorrect | • Identify the error.<br>• Explain the rationale behind the student's error.<br>• How would you help them "unlearn" the misconception?<br>• Solve the problem correctly.<br>• Explain how to solve the problem correctly. |

# CHECKING FOR UNDERSTANDING

Teachers should have clear intentions about what it is that they want students to learn before deciding the type of worked example and prompt to use. Look back at the module, and apply what you learned by creating three worked examples in the tables below.

| | CORRECT WORKED EXAMPLE (✓) |
|---|---|
| **Step 1:**<br>Choose a grade- or content-level standard. | |
| **Step 2:**<br>Develop one learning intention and its success criteria from the standard. | |
| **Step 3:**<br>Find or create one problem that aligns with the learning intention and success criteria above in Step 2. | |
| **Step 4:**<br>Solve the problem fully and correctly, showing every step. | |

## CORRECT WORKED EXAMPLE
### (✓)

| | |
|---|---|
| **Step 5:**<br>Select a prompt that focuses on developing students' conceptual understanding. | <br><br><br><br> |
| **Step 6:**<br>Finalize the problem by including a student name in the prompt and clearly marking it as a correct worked example with a checkmark (✓). | <br><br><br><br> |

## PARTIALLY COMPLETE WORKED EXAMPLE
### (✓)

| | |
|---|---|
| **Step 1:**<br>Choose a grade- or content-level standard. | <br><br><br><br> |
| **Step 2:**<br>Develop one learning intention and its success criteria from the standard. | <br><br><br><br> |
| **Step 3:**<br>Anticipate learning challenges, and identify one "sticky point" in the problem-solving process. | <br><br><br><br> |

*(Continued)*

(Continued)

| PARTIALLY COMPLETE WORKED EXAMPLE (✓) | |
|---|---|
| **Step 4:**<br><br>Find or create one problem that aligns with the learning intention and success criteria and addresses the "sticky point" in Step 3. | _____<br><br>_____<br><br>_____<br><br>_____ |
| **Step 5:**<br><br>Solve the problem correctly and until the point where students may get "stuck" in the problem-solving process. | _____<br><br>_____<br><br>_____<br><br>_____ |
| **Step 6:**<br><br>Select a prompt that focuses on developing students' conceptual understanding. | _____<br><br>_____<br><br>_____<br><br>_____ |
| **Step 7:**<br><br>Fiinalize the problem by including a student name in the prompt and clearly indicating it as a partially correct worked example with a half checkmark (✓). | _____<br><br>_____<br><br>_____<br><br>_____ |

| INCORRECT WORKED EXAMPLE (X) | |
|---|---|
| **Step 1:**<br><br>Choose a grade- or content-level standard. | _____<br><br>_____<br><br>_____<br><br>_____ |

| INCORRECT WORKED EXAMPLE (X) | |
|---|---|
| **Step 2:**<br><br>Develop one learning intention and its success criteria from the standard. | _____<br><br>_____<br><br>_____<br><br>_____ |
| **Step 3:**<br><br>List common errors or misconceptions. Then select one to be the focus. | _____<br><br>_____<br><br>_____<br><br>_____ |
| **Step 4:**<br><br>Find or create one problem that aligns with the learning intention and success criteria and addresses the one common error in Step 3. | _____<br><br>_____<br><br>_____<br><br>_____ |
| **Step 5:**<br><br>Solve the problem fully and incorrectly with the common error. | _____<br><br>_____<br><br>_____<br><br>_____ |
| **Step 6:**<br><br>Select a prompt that focuses on the error to develop students' conceptual understanding. | _____<br><br>_____<br><br>_____<br><br>_____ |
| **Step 7:**<br><br>Finalize the problem by including a student name in the prompt and clearly indicating it as an incorrect worked example with an "X." | _____<br><br>_____<br><br>_____<br><br>_____ |

# Exit Ticket

Take a moment and self-evaluate your learning in this module using these statements.

1. I can identify the three types of worked examples.

| 1 | 2 | 3 | 4 | 5 |
|---|---|---|---|---|
| Strongly disagree | Disagree | Neutral | Agree | Strongly agree |

Explain the reason for your selection.

_____

_____

2. I can explain the differences between each type of worked example.

| 1 | 2 | 3 | 4 | 5 |
|---|---|---|---|---|
| Strongly disagree | Disagree | Neutral | Agree | Strongly agree |

Explain the reason for your selection.

_____

_____

3. I can create worked examples to use in my mathematics instruction.

| 1 | 2 | 3 | 4 | 5 |
|---|---|---|---|---|
| Strongly disagree | Disagree | Neutral | Agree | Strongly agree |

Explain the reason for your selection.

_____

_____

# MODULE 10

# How Do I Scaffold Mathematics Tasks in My Classroom?

Before we jump into our topic for this module, let's activate our prior knowledge for this section.

---

## BIG IDEA #3

Take a moment and flip back to p. 6. Rewrite **Big Idea #3,** and fill in the blank.

**Big Idea #3:** Mathematics teaching and learning must . . . _____

_____.

---

Look back at Module #7 on pp. 115–119. What are the elements that separate a mathematics task from a rigorous one?

_____

_____

_____

_____

# MODULE #10

**Learning Intention**

We are learning how to design and incorporate scaffolding so that they engage and support students through the productive struggle embedded in rigorous mathematical tasks.

**Success Criteria**

We'll know we've learned this when we can:

1.  describe the model for *how scaffolding works*,

2.  explain how teachers can scaffold the mathematical teaching and learning process, and

3.  explain how students can participate in scaffolding the mathematical teaching and learning process.

There is no such thing as a rigorous mathematics task without productive struggle. Studies suggest that struggling to make sense of mathematics is a necessary component in learning and understanding its concepts, procedures, and ideas (Barlow et al., 2018; Hiebert & Grouws, 2007). The National Council of Teachers of Mathematics (NCTM, 2014) also supports the notion of productive struggle as one of its eight effective mathematics teaching practices. Teachers and students, especially in the beginning, may feel uncomfortable when faced with these moments, interpret them as unnecessary roadblocks to learning, or try to avoid them altogether. Instead, when students are confused, can't make sense of an answer, or reach an impasse, teachers can (Warshauer, 2015):

*   explicitly remind them that their struggle is an important and natural part of learning,

*   acknowledge students' consternation,

*   encourage perseverance,

*   ask questions, and

*   offer time to work through problems.

Reflect on your mathematics teaching and your students' mathematics learning. What is your approach to designing scaffolds for productive struggle? Jot these questions down in the space below so that we can revisit them throughout our work in this Playbook.

_____

_____

_____

_____

# SCAFFOLDS: THE RIGHT KIND OF STRUGGLE

It is not enough to design meaningful and relevant experiences if students don't struggle enough or too much. Dale and Scherrer (2015) called this the "Goldilocks Discourse": Too much scaffolding constrains students' opportunities to learn how to persevere in solving challenging tasks, enough scaffolding leads to student frustration and unsystematic exploration, and just the right amount lets students productively struggle with content that they otherwise could not access. When we look closely at "struggling" and "struggling productively," the difference between the two lies in the strategic moments of temporary access to the cognitive demand.

Wood et al. (1976) initially introduced the term and defined it as "a process that enables a child or novice to solve a task or achieve a goal that would be beyond his unassisted efforts" (p. 90). In addition, Wood et al. identified six scaffolding functions or features within different phases of a lesson (see Figure 10.1).

**FIGURE 10.1** ● Six functions of scaffolding.

| FUNCTION | DESCRIPTION |
|---|---|
| Recruitment | The teacher solicits students' interest in the task, ensures that they see relevance in the activity or assignment, and understand the requirements of the task. |
| Reduction in Degrees of Freedom | Teachers simplify the task by reducing the number of acts or steps to reach a solution. They engage in task analysis, understand the steps and process, which can be used to reduce the options and allow a focus on the steps required to be successful. |
| Direction Maintenance | The teacher guides students so they do not head in the wrong direction, lose interest, or give up. |
| Marking Critical Features | Teachers highlight some features of the task, like noting actions that had an impact so that the learner is likely to try that again and noting the discrepancy between what the learner did and what might be a more correct response. |
| Frustration Control | The instructor provides "face-saving" comments for the student who is struggling or offers additional prompts and cues that support success. Be mindful not to create too much dependency on the one offering the scaffolds. |
| Demonstration | Allow the student an opportunity to imitate the actions of another through modeling, thinking aloud, and providing other types of input. This may resolve the temporary block in the successful completion of the task. |

**Source:** Description of functions and other descriptions based on the work of Wood et al. (1976). Adapted from Frey, Fisher, and Almarode (2023).

Scaffolding is a supporting framework with three key aspects to the relationship between it and the specific task at hand (Frey, Fisher, & Almarode, 2023):

1. Scaffolding is only used when the task at hand is not possible to complete with that support system or structure.

2. Scaffolding is customized (i.e., moveable) based on the specific needs of the individuals engaged in the task; there is no one-size-fits-all scaffolding.

3. Scaffolding is used until the support system or structure is no longer needed; scaffolds are temporary and not permanent.

The model of *how scaffolding works* in Figure 10.2 considers every phase involved in the mathematical teaching and learning process, from start to finish (Frey, Fisher, & Almarode, 2023). There are five aspects to the model, as follows:

- **Mental Model:** These are essential to our understanding of complex content, practices, processes, and ideas. They represent what we are aiming for or what proficiency and mastery look like for a particular concept, skill, or understanding. We must develop and share a clear representation of what students are working toward in learning for scaffolding to work.

- **Goal Setting:** Scaffolding works when we identify where students are in their learning journey and make a relative comparison between their current location and the mental model. Then we set measurable and attainable goals to move forward in their learning. Without this, scaffolding will not be temporary and it won't work.

- **Learning Task and Practice:** Practice is one of the most important contingencies in scaffolding. It grows our learning, promotes conceptual development, improves our skills, and enhances our understanding. There is no improvement if we don't engage in certain types of practice, and not all practice is the same.

- **Front-End, Distributed, Peer, and Back-End Scaffolding:** There are four types of scaffolding. *Front-end scaffolds* are enacted in advance of the learning; *distributed scaffolds* are implemented, monitored, and adjusted during the learning process; *peer scaffolding* is when peers learn to support the learning; and *back-end scaffolds* are used after the learning tasks are done. We will focus on these in this module.

- **Fade:** This involves decreasing the amount or type of scaffolding needed to complete a task or activity. Scaffolds are temporary, and they are removed to transfer the ownership of learning back to the student.

**FIGURE 10.2** ● Model for how scaffolding works with guiding questions.

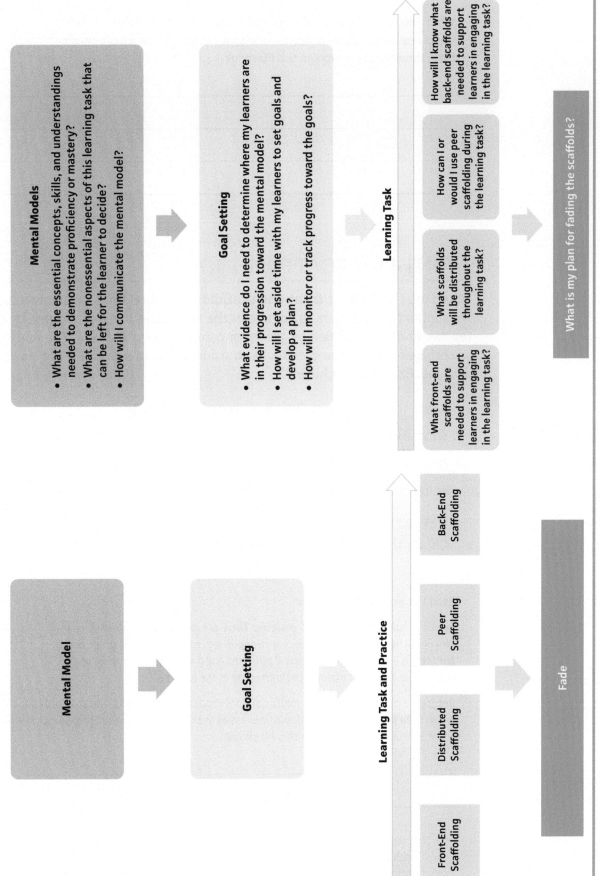

**Source:** Reprinted from Frey, Fisher, and Almarode (2023).

What thoughts or questions do you have about the model for *how scaffolding works*? Jot them down in the space below so that we can revisit them throughout our work in this Playbook.

_____

_____

_____

_____

## FRONT-END SCAFFOLDING

When we think about front-end scaffolds, we need to ask ourselves how we support our learners to engage in the task. They are determined by the teacher and are informed by grade- or course-level standards. The scaffolds are bridges to more complex tasks so students are prepared for the learning to come. Examples include:

- Share the learning intention and success criteria.

- Simplify a task.

- Assess prerequisite skills and background knowledge.

- Refine current skills and knowledge.

- Frontload vocabulary.

- Chunk the text into smaller sections.

Read the word problem below.

*Sandra is holding a bag with 20 marbles. There are red, yellow, and green marbles in the bag. She has a greater chance of pulling red marble than a green one, but there is a low chance that she will pull a red one over a yellow one. How many red, yellow, and green marbles could there be in the bag?*

Before we present this to our middle school students, what front-end scaffolds should we include in this lesson? Jot down your ideas in the space below so that we can revisit them throughout our work in this Playbook.

_____

_____

_____

_____

# DISTRIBUTED SCAFFOLDING

Teachers provide distributed scaffolds while students engage with the rigorous mathematical learning task and should be careful not to inadvertently reduce the cognitive demand. Dixon (2018) described these just-in-time scaffolds as ones provided to students before they attempt a challenging task and when their struggle becomes unproductive or unable to move forward without help. They are harder to plan for in advance because they are used in response to learner's needs in the moment. With that said, we should still make time beforehand to consider ways to support students based on their individual and group needs, common mistakes, and our experience in teaching the content (Frey, Fisher, & Almarode, 2023). Examples include:

- Highlight key ideas.

- Pause to summarize and synthesize information being presented.

- Pose questions to check for understanding (see Figure 10.3).

- Prompt with statements or questions to focus on the cognitive or metacognitive processes needed to complete the task (see Figures 10.4 and 10.5).

**FIGURE 10.3** ● Types of questions for distributed scaffolding.

| TYPE OF QUESTION | DESCRIPTION |
| --- | --- |
| Elicitation questions | Elicitation questions invite the learner to offer information using concepts or skills that have been previously taught.<br><br>This type of question is often phrased using familiar questioning words: *who, what, when, where, why, and how.* They are used to unearth misconceptions and check for factual knowledge. |
| Elaboration questions | Elaboration questions often follow an initial elicitation as the teacher further probes student understanding. These questions are intended to increase the length of the response and allow students to do some thinking. Often, explaining thinking helps both the speaker and the listener to figure out what went wrong. |
| Clarification questions | As with elaboration questions, these are frequently paired with initial elicitation questions and are intended to further expose the student's knowledge of the content. These questions allow the teacher to gain further details about students' understanding. |
| Divergent questions | Divergent questions require the learner to consolidate concepts about two topics to create a new relationship. The teacher's intent in this case is to discover how the student uses existing knowledge to formulate a new understanding. |
| Heuristic questions | Sometimes the focus of the question is on students' ability to formulate an informal problem-solving technique. Heuristics, also described as a rule of thumb, are techniques learners use as they address and solve a problem. |
| Inventive questions | These questions invite students to use what they have learned to speculate or create. They stimulate imaginative throught and can unearth misconceptions. |

**Source:** Reprinted from Frey, Fisher, and Almarode (2023).

**FIGURE 10.4** ● Types of prompts for distributed scaffolding.

| TYPE OF PROMPT | DEFINITION/WHEN TO USE |
|---|---|
| Background knowledge | Used when there is content that the student has already known, has been taught, or has experienced but has temporarily forgotten or is using incorrectly. |
| Process or procedure | Used when established or generally agreed-on rules or guidelines are not being followed and a reminder will help resolve the error or misconception. |
| Reflective | Used to encourage students to be metacognitive and to think about their thinking, which can then be used to determine the next steps or the solution to a problem. |
| Heuristic | Used to help learners develop their own way to solve problems. These are informal problem-solving procedures. They do not have to be the same as others' heuristics, but they do need to work. |

**Source:** Adapted from Frey, Fisher, and Almarode (2023).

**FIGURE 10.5** ● Types of cues for distributed scaffolding.

| TYPE OF CUE | DEFINITION |
|---|---|
| Visual | A range of graphic hints that guide students through thinking or understanding. |
| Verbal | Variation in speech is used to draw attention to something specific or verbal attention-getters that focus students' thinking. |
| Gestural/ Physical | The teacher's body movements or motions are used to draw attention to something that has been missed. |
| Environmental | Using the surroundings, and things in the surroundings, to influence students' understanding. |

**Source:** Adapted from Frey, Fisher, and Almarode (2023).

Analyze the sample problem below. What potential distributed scaffolds might students need? What questions, prompts, and cues would support their productive struggle? Jot down your ideas and questions in the spaces below so that we can revisit them throughout our work in this Playbook.

Look at the four equations below. Which one stands out from the rest and why? Can you come up with a rationale for why each one could be considered unique?

$$y = -\frac{3}{2}x + 4$$
$$-4x = 6y$$
$$6x + 4y = -4$$
$$y - 5 = \frac{2}{3}(x - 6)$$

| QUESTIONS | PROMPTS | CUES |
|---|---|---|
| _____ | _____ | _____ |
| _____ | _____ | _____ |
| _____ | _____ | _____ |
| _____ | _____ | _____ |

# PEER SCAFFOLDING

Peer scaffolding refers to the collaborative moves that peers make to aid novices in accomplishing content or linguistic tasks that they would otherwise be unable to achieve individually (Devos, 2015). Teachers are not the only ones who offer scaffolding; students begin to support each other when they are a regular part of their learning experience, even if they are not formally taught how to do so (Frey, Fisher, & Almarode, 2023). They adopt "teacher moves" with their peers, using cognitive supports like questions, prompts, and cues and emotional supports when faced with productive struggle.

If we want to create positive and safe learning environments, then students need to foster positive relationships among each other. Meyer and Turner (2007) described emotional scaffolds as reliable and temporary teacher-initiated interactions that support students' positive emotional experiences to achieve a variety of classroom goals. However, there is no reason why students can't provide these types of support for each other. One example of peer emotional scaffolding is called "RULER" and comes from the Yale Center for Emotional Intelligence (Yale University, 2022; www.ruler approach.org). RULER includes five areas: Recognizing, Understanding, Labeling, Expressing, and Regulating emotions. After some coaching and guidance, students use these strategies and the tools that they have been taught so they can provide emotional scaffolding for one another.

Think about the student-to-student relationships in your classroom. How would you describe their interactions among themselves? How engaged and supportive are they of each other during mathematical discourse? Jot down your observations in the space below so that we can revisit them throughout our work in this Playbook.

_____

_____

_____

_____

A more structured approach to peer scaffolding is peer tutoring. It is a more formal and structured approach and has an effect size of 0.54 on the one receiving the tutoring and an effect size of 0.48 on the one doing the tutoring (visiblelearningmetax.com). Research shows that both parties significantly benefit from these models. Here are six versions that can be adapted to the mathematical classroom:

1.  **Classwide Peer Tutoring (CWPT).** Students work in groups of two to five students, and each one has an opportunity to be both the tutee and the tutor. The goal is to practice or review skills and content rather than to introduce new learning. The teacher typically assigns the content, which includes a peer explaining the work, asking questions of the group, and providing feedback to the peer(s). CWPT involves structured procedures and direct rehearsal and may include competitive teams with the scores posted (Maheady et al., 2001).

2.  **Same-Age Peer Tutoring.** This is similar to classwide peer tutoring (CWPT), except not all students are engaged in tutoring at the same time. This structure is flexible so that tutoring may occur within the same classroom or with students in different classrooms. Again, the teacher trains the tutors on their roles and establishes routines for same-age tutoring (Frey, Fisher, & Almarode, 2023).

3.  **Cross-Age Peer Tutoring.** Older students are paired with younger students, and the older students have the responsibility to serve as the tutor. Tutors explain concepts, model appropriate behavior, ask questions, and encourage better study habits. Tutors may even be taught to design lessons for their younger students (e.g., Jacobson et al., 2001).

4.  **Peer-Assisted Learning Strategies (PALS).** Teachers train students to use a series of coaching strategies. Learners work in pairs and take turns tutoring and being tutored. Tutors use the questioning techniques to help peers think through mathematical concepts and skills (D. Fuchs et al., 2000; L. S. Fuchs et al., 1999).

5.  **Reciprocal Peer Tutoring (RPT).** Students are paired randomly. Each partnership is responsible for synthesizing content, preparing tasks, and asking questions, complete with answers and explanations. Often students develop practice tests during RPT and then identify areas of additional learning needed (e.g., Alegre-Ansuategui et al., 2017).

6.  **Teach-Back.** Ha Dinh et al. (2016) introduced this as an approach to increase patients' adherence to medical advice. Since then, it has been adapted for the PK–12 educational setting so students reframe their learning and teach others (Fisher et al., 2021). Providing them with opportunities to teach back what they have learned is good for their learning, and it's a great opportunity for determining what has stuck and if there are any misconceptions. Students teach back to the class or directly to the teacher, and they are encouraged to go beyond

the classroom and teach their siblings, parents, or extended family members. The key is to ensure that the same students are not always doing the teach-back. Everyone needs an opportunity as it is good for learning and for assessment.

Let's take a moment TO pause and process our learning. List the ways that you encourage peer scaffolding now and ways that you want to develop this further. Jot down your thoughts in the spaces below so that we can revisit them throughout our work in this Playbook.

| PEER SCAFFOLDING | WHAT I DO NOW | WHAT I WANT TO DO |
|---|---|---|
| Emotional Scaffolds | | |
| Cognitive Scaffolds | | |

## BACK-END SCAFFOLDING

Unlike the three other scaffolds, back-end scaffolds uniquely take place after the learning experience occurred. They are used to:

- correct misconceptions or errors,

- provide feedback to go beyond the learning, and

- solidify student's understanding of mathematical skills, concepts, or knowledge (Frey, Fisher, et al., 2023).

One example of a back-end scaffold is a graphic organizer. Although it can be used as a front-end scaffolding tool, research shows that its impact greatly increases when it is used after lessons. When graphic organizers are generically used in the lesson, the effect size is 0.61, but when they are used after, the effect size is 1.84 (Englert & Mariage, 1991). There are four types of graphic organizers (see Figure 10.6), but as a back-end scaffold, we ask students to take what they learned and compare and contrast it with other mathematical ideas. This technique is not simply used to document what happened; it is an intermediate tool for something else, mostly discussion and writing (Fisher & Frey, 2018).

**FIGURE 10.6** ● Four types of graphic organizers.

| FUNCTION | TYPES |
|---|---|
| Outline | • Timeline<br>• Semantic maps<br>• Flow chart<br>• Sequence chart<br>• Spider map<br>• Cycle map |
| Compare-contrast | • Matrix<br>• Venn<br>• T-chart |
| Hierarchical | • Tree diagram<br>• Thematic map<br>• Fishbone map |
| Relational | • Bubble map<br>• Semantic feature analysis<br>• Problem-solution |

**Source:** Adapted from Frey, Fisher, and Almarode (2023).

Another back-end scaffold is to offer feedback. Again, teachers do this as a distributed scaffold as the learning is happening, but in this context, we want to use it as a means to address student misconceptions or errors (Frey, Fisher, et al., 2023). Feedback comes in at least three forms, as follows (Vrabie, 2021):

- **Appreciation:** Recognizing and rewarding someone for their work. This connects and motivates people, and it's vital since intrinsic motivation is one of the critical factors for high performance.

- **Coaching:** Helping someone expand their knowledge, skills, and capabilities. It is also an opportunity to address feelings, which helps balance and strengthen relationships.

- **Evaluation:** Assessing someone against a set of standards, aligning expectations, and informing decision-making.

Let's apply it to an upcoming rigorous mathematical task. Identify one that you plan to use with your students. Use the guiding questions to identify ways to incorporate the four types of scaffolding. Jot them down in the space below so that we can revisit them throughout our work in this Playbook.

| SCAFFOLD | GUIDING QUESTION | POTENTIAL TEACHER OR STUDENT MOVES |
| --- | --- | --- |
| Front-End Scaffolding | What front-end scaffolds are needed to support learners in engaging in the learning task? | _____  _____  _____  _____ |
| Distributed Scaffolding | What scaffolds will be distributed throughout the learning task? | _____  _____  _____  _____ |
| Peer Scaffolding | How can I or would I use peer scaffolding during the learning task? | _____  _____  _____  _____ |
| Back-End Scaffolding | How will I know what back-end scaffolds are needed to support learners in engaging in the learning task? | _____  _____  _____  _____ |

# Exit Ticket

Take a moment and self-evaluate your learning in this module using these statements.

1. I can describe the model for *how scaffolding works*.

| 1 | 2 | 3 | 4 | 5 |
|---|---|---|---|---|
| Strongly disagree | Disagree | Neutral | Agree | Strongly agree |

Explain the reason for your selection.

_____

_____

2. I can explain how teachers can scaffold the mathematical teaching and learning process.

| 1 | 2 | 3 | 4 | 5 |
|---|---|---|---|---|
| Strongly disagree | Disagree | Neutral | Agree | Strongly agree |

Explain the reason for your selection.

_____

_____

3. I can explain how students can scaffold the mathematical teaching and learning process.

| 1 | 2 | 3 | 4 | 5 |
|---|---|---|---|---|
| Strongly disagree | Disagree | Neutral | Agree | Strongly agree |

Explain the reason for your selection.

_____

_____

## MODULE 11

# How Do I Integrate Deliberate Practice Into My Classroom?

Before we step to far into this module, take a moment and flip back to the scaffolding model on p. 151. You will notice that practice plays a role in our model of scaffolding. Now, look just above the images of the models to the section that describes each component of the scaffolding process. What does it say about practice? Using the space below, answer the following question: What is the role of practice in teaching and learning mathematics? Be very specific!

_____

_____

_____

_____

Now, let's continue to lay the foundation for this module by recalling the elements of mathematics teaching and learning. There are five of them. Flip back to Module #1 of this Playbook if you need a quick reminder. Write those five elements in the left column of the chart; each element gets its own row.

| ELEMENT OF MATHEMATICS TEACHING AND LEARNING | WAYS TO PRACTICE |
|---|---|
| 1. | _____<br>_____<br>_____<br>_____ |
| 2. | _____<br>_____<br>_____<br>_____ |
| 3. | _____<br>_____<br>_____<br>_____ |
| 4. | _____<br>_____<br>_____<br>_____ |
| 5. | _____<br>_____<br>_____<br>_____ |

You have already noticed that the column on the right asks for your ideas about "ways to practice" that element. Take some time to generate ideas for practice, or list the ways you get learners to practice in your mathematics classroom. By the way, ideas may go in more than one row.

The ideas you generated or shared in the right column of that chart is where we will focus our attention. There are three points that we hope to extract from this module. They are as follows:

1. Practice is necessary and essential in developing conceptual knowledge, procedural fluency, strategic competence, adaptive reasoning, and productive dispositions.

2. Not all practice is the same. Different types of practice yield different outcomes.

3. The desire to practice is not always there for learners. Learners often have to be motivated to practice.

So, let's unpack each of these points.

# MODULE #11

**Learning Intention**

We are learning about the relationship between practice and mathematics teaching and learning.

**Success Criteria**

We'll know we've learned this when we can:

1. compare and contrast the different types of practice in our mathematics classrooms,

2. explain the differences between productive and unproductive success and failure in mathematics,

3. describe the three characteristics of effective deliberate practice in mathematics, and

4. use different techniques to motivate learners to engage in deliberate mathematics practice.

# THE ROLE OF PRACTICE

There are several sayings linked to the idea of practice. "Practice makes perfect" is one of those sayings and is completely wrong—misleading at best. Instead, practice makes permanent. What we must discern in our mathematics teaching is what exactly are we seeking to make permanent? The answer to that question helps us create and implement specific practice opportunities that foster, nurture, and sustain mathematics learning for all our learners. The specific practice opportunities we provide for our learners are based on the specific learning outcomes and whether they engage in those opportunities for practice.

Flip back to your work in Modules #2 and #3. Place a sticky note, tab, or something that allows you to flip back and forth between your analysis of the standards, the learning progression you developed for a particular unit, and your work in this module. We are going to begin to develop opportunities for practice based on that work.

Remember point #2 on p. 163. Not all practice is the _____ . Together, we will walk through how to decide which type of practice gives us the greatest potential for making learning permanent.

To be very honest, practice in mathematics has rightfully earned itself a terrible reputation. When someone mentions practice in mathematics, what immediately pops into your mind? Mindless handouts, countless repetitive problems, and the stamina required to just get it done. Furthermore, we often make the mistake of grading the practice, not giving feedback, which negates the idea of practice. We will devote the next module to feedback, so hold on to that idea for now. In fact, to really lock in this relationship, fill in the statement below with the terms "practice" in the first blank and "feedback" in the second blank.

_____ requires

_____!

## NOT ALL PRACTICE IS THE SAME

There are two things to consider with practice. First, practice makes permanent, not perfect. If learners engage in a practice opportunity but solve 4,345,987 problems the wrong way, that is what they will learn—the wrong way. If learners engage in 4,345,987 problems that simply require the repeated use of an algorithm, that is what they will learn—the algorithm, not conceptual knowledge, strategic competence, adaptive reasoning, or productive dispositions. Therefore, we must develop and provide *deliberate* practice opportunities that are *scaffolded* for our learners. Without deliberate practice opportunities with sufficient scaffolds, practice opportunities will not move learning forward and prevent us from fading the scaffolding.

Return to Module #10 where we spent time learning about scaffolding in mathematics. We want to blend scaffolding and feedback with our work from Modules #2 and #3. You should have those marked and ready to go.

Using the space below, what are some scaffolds that might be useful in ensuring that learners are supported in their practice opportunities within the standard or unit you mapped out in Modules #2 and #3? The chart will help you organize your potential scaffolds into front-end, distributed, peer, and back-end scaffolds.

| POTENTIAL FRONT-END SCAFFOLDS | POTENTIAL DISTRIBUTED SCAFFOLDS | POTENTIAL PEER SCAFFOLDS | POTENTIAL BACK-END SCAFFOLDS |
|---|---|---|---|
| _____ | _____ | _____ | _____ |
| _____ | _____ | _____ | _____ |
| _____ | _____ | _____ | _____ |
| _____ | _____ | _____ | _____ |

Second, not all practice is the same. What type of practice is most effective in the teaching and learning of mathematics? Are their different ways to practice conceptual knowledge, procedural fluency, strategic competence, adaptive reasoning, and productive dispositions? The following three scenarios may help clarify the answers to these two questions:

Scenario #1

Every morning, a group of students gathers in the school's media center to play chess. The students rotate who plays who and simply play every day from the time the first bus drops off students at the school until the bell rings, signaling the start of homeroom.

Scenario #2

Zamari does not just arbitrarily select a chess opponent in the morning. He seeks out individuals that frequently win their chess matches. His goal is to reduce the number of moves to checkmate. So, while playing with an opponent he assesses as being "better at chess," he studies the moves of his opponent and reflects on his performance after each match. He often asks questions during the match to get information about what his opponent was thinking when they made a certain move.

Scenario #3

Ava's uncle is a competitive chess player. While not in the top 1,000, her uncle is considered an expert relative to Ava. Ava's uncle will set up different board configurations and analyzes Ava's decisions and moves within those configurations. Her uncle coaches her and teaches her various techniques or approaches to different chess board configurations.

> In the space below, identify the similarities and differences between these three scenarios. What do you notice about these three scenarios?
>
> _____
>
> _____
>
> _____
>
> _____

Just as there were three scenarios above, there are three different types of practices: naïve, purposeful, and deliberate (Ericsson & Pool, 2016). In the table below, each of the three types of practice are listed, along with a summary of that type of practice. Use the space in the right column to come up with examples from your experiences for each type of practice.

| TYPE OF PRACTICE | DEFINITION | MY EXAMPLES |
|---|---|---|
| Naïve practice | Going through the motions; repetition of the task with no goal | _____<br><br>_____<br><br>_____<br><br>_____ |
| Purposeful practice | Goal-directed, focused, includes feedback, and is challenging | _____<br><br>_____<br><br>_____<br><br>_____ |

| TYPE OF PRACTICE | DEFINITION | MY EXAMPLES |
|---|---|---|
| Deliberate practice | In addition to the aspects of purposeful practice, there is a defined expertise, and a teacher provides guidance activities | _____ _____ _____ _____ |

Take a moment and return to the three scenarios involving chess players. Label each scenario based on the type of practice (e.g., naïve, purposeful, and deliberate) presented in that scenario.

Reflect on all the practice opportunities you offer your learners in your mathematics classroom. If all those practice opportunities represent 100%, what percentage of those opportunities represent naïve practice, purposeful practice, and deliberate practice? Use the fraction bar below to visually represent your response. We have provided an example for you.

Our Example:

| Naïve Practice = 40% | Purposeful Practice = 20% | Deliberate Practice = 35% |
|---|---|---|

Your Response:

|  |  |  |
|---|---|---|

## MERGING DELIBERATE PRACTICE AND SCAFFOLDING IN MATHEMATICS

Take a moment, and in the space provided, redraw the model of scaffolding we have included in this Playbook. Only this time, make it mathematics specific. Rather than labeling the first part of the model as "Mental Model," describe the mental models you would create to support learners in the particular standard and learning progression from Modules #2 and #3.

*(Continued)*

(Continued)

Oh, if you need scaffolding to redraw the model of scaffolding, flip back to p. 151 in Module #10. Remember, be mathematics specific.

_____

_____

_____

_____

_____

_____

_____

_____

_____

Practice and scaffolding are tightly connected in mathematics teaching and learning. Take a look at the following statements regarding this tight connection:

- Once we, together with our learners, have developed a mental model of mathematics learning for a particular standard, unit, or lesson sequence, we must determine where learners are in their conceptual knowledge, procedural fluency, strategic competence, adaptive reasoning, and productive dispositions.

- The "difference" between where learners are in the progression and the mental model tells us and our learners where deliberate practice is needed.

- By setting goals, we develop a plan for implementing deliberate practice across the entire standard, unit, or lesson sequence.

- We must scaffold those deliberate practice sessions because the very nature of this type of practice is to move outside of learners' comfort zones.

- Feedback before, during, and after deliberate practice helps us and our students make informed decisions about when to fade a particular scaffold.

To build the bridge between practice and scaffolding, let's consider the practice of musicians. There are significant differences between you, me, and

Martha Argerich or Daniel Barenboim. Those last two individuals are the world's most sought-after classical pianists. As amateurs and casual piano players, we typically engage in naïve practice, perhaps practicing only when we have a few minutes of downtime. While we may enjoy playing the piano, we are probably not goal focused and rarely have the intent of developing expertise beyond what is required to simply enjoy playing hit songs. Now consider Ginevra, an 11-year-old, Italian music student who loves to play the piano and plans to play professionally. She has clear goals and is very focused on learning note values, rests, and chord progressions (i.e., primary chords, secondary chords, and circle progressions). She has peers video record her so that she can watch and listen to her performance, analyze her execution of music, and find areas for improvement. This is after she has watched her idol, Martha Argerich, play the same piece. In other words, she engages in purposeful practice. She knows what expert players do, and her piano teacher provides her with specific guidance on the skills she needs to improve in playing a particular piece. Therefore, they customize her practice to address those skills. In this case, Ginevra is engaged in deliberate practice.

As Ericsson and Pool (2016) stated, "We are drawing a clear distinction between purposeful practice—in which a person tries very hard to push himself or herself to improve—and practice that is both purposeful and informed. In particular, deliberate practice is informed and guided by the best performers' accomplishments and by an understanding of what these expert performers do to excel. Deliberate practice is purposeful practice that knows where it is going and how to get there" (p. 1759).

Return to your response to the question at the beginning of this module. That question was as follows:

1. What is the role of practice in teaching and learning mathematics?

After learning about the three different types of practice, please select a different color or pen or pencil to revise or edit your earlier responses. What would you add to your response? What might need revising based on your new understanding of naïve, purposeful, and deliberate practice?

_____

_____

_____

_____

Now let's add a second question to consider: What allowed you to fade the supports in a scaffolded learning experience?

_____

_____

# GETTING LEARNERS TO ENGAGE IN DELIBERATE PRACTICE

Deliberate practice is required for teacher fading and increased learner responsibility through scaffolding. There is considerable research on deliberate practice. For example, across three meta-analyses, there are 161 studies, including 13,689 students, resulting in 316 effects (www.visiblelearningmetax.com). Together, the average weighted effect size is 0.49. This type of practice has the potential to accelerate student learning. But there is a catch.

If you look at the essential characteristics of deliberate practice as identified by Ericsson and Pool (2016), one or two characteristics likely do not sit well with learners. Can you guess which ones? Circle the specific characteristics that might be barriers to your mathematics learners participating in deliberate practice:

1. Set a goal.

2. Make time for a distraction-free focused practice.

3. Ensure you will have access to immediate feedback.

4. Push yourself outside of your comfort zone.

> Why did you circle that characteristic or those characteristics? What evidence do you have to support your choice?
>
> _____
>
> _____
>
> _____
>
> _____

Students rarely engage in deliberate practice. However, we share some, if not most, of the blame for this one. As we have mentioned, the dread of homework is on us. If we equate practice, much like homework, with the completion of one gazillion problems, that is not motivating, engaging, or effective for learning. Many of the practice opportunities or tasks offered to our mathematics learners require nothing more than naïve practice. The other reason students rarely engage in deliberate practice is that deliberate practice is challenging. Students may actively try to avoid deliberate practice, opting for the more comfortable, less challenging naïve practice. When students simply go through the motions to please their teachers, they will not realize the powerful impact of deliberate practice. As we shall see, having goals, pushing past your comfort zone, responding to feedback, understanding what expertise looks like, and accepting the challenge are all important aspects of deliberate practice, practice that requires scaffolding.

There's that connection to scaffolding. Take a moment and return to p. 168 where we looked at the connection between practice and scaffolding. You may need to review those statements again. Afterward, summarize the relationship between practice and scaffolding in your classroom.

_____

_____

_____

_____

So, how do we increase deliberate practice opportunities and motivate learners to engage in those opportunities?

## MOTIVATING LEARNERS TO ENGAGE IN DELIBERATE PRACTICE

Take a moment and reflect on practice opportunities, deliberate practice opportunities that were successful in your mathematics classroom. In other words, those deliberate practice opportunities that learners engaged in and benefited from by moving their learning forward across all elements of mathematics teaching and learning. How were these opportunities different from those that were not successful? Jot down your response in the space below.

_____

_____

_____

_____

When looking for research on how to motivate learners to practice, we can look at our school gymnasium. This area of research is well known in physical education. Block (1995), Hastie et al. (2013), and Tjeerdsma (1995) highlighted three essential characteristics of practice tasks that motivate learners to engage in deliberate practice:

1. Success oriented

2. Autonomy supportive

3. Developmentally appropriate

This specific example shows how collaboration across our schools can enhance teaching and learning for all of us. Let's learn a bit more from our physical education colleagues about how they get their learners to engage in deliberate practice.

*Success Oriented.* Learners will struggle to find the motivation to engage in practice, specifically deliberate practice, if they do not experience success. If our learners never experience success, we certainly cannot expect them to link deliberate practice and moving forward in their learning. As a learner, if every task, activity, or experience results in a sense of failure, we must develop and provide deliberate practice opportunities that allow learners to experience success.

As we move through the final modules of this Playbook, we will continue to rely on the work we did in Modules #2 and #3. As before, grab the concepts, skills, and practices you focused on in that particular standard, unit, or learning sequence. By the way, we hope you have selected the same standard, unit, or learning sequence throughout this entire Playbook. In just a few more modules, we hope this leaves you and your colleagues with a comprehensive plan! Now, back to our work in making deliberate practice *success oriented*. Write the concepts, skills, and understandings in the left column. We'll move to the column on the right in just a second. For now, just focus on that left column. We have provided two examples for you: *two-digit subtraction with regrouping and constructing a mathematical argument.*

| CONCEPTS, SKILLS, AND DISPOSITIONS | WAYS TO ADAPT OR SCAFFOLD |
|---|---|
| *Example: two-digit subtraction with regrouping* | • *Size of each digit*<br>• *Access to manipulatives*<br>• *Choice of strategy (e.g., drawing)*<br>• *Whether the learning experience or task is done independently, with a partner, or in a group* |

| CONCEPTS, SKILLS, AND DISPOSITIONS | WAYS TO ADAPT OR SCAFFOLD |
|---|---|
| *Example: constructing a mathematical argument* | • *The type of problem*<br>• *How the argument is presented (e.g., written, verbally)*<br>• *Whether the learning experience or task is done independently, with a partner, or in a group* |
| _____<br>_____<br>_____ | _____<br>_____<br>_____ |
| _____<br>_____<br>_____ | _____<br>_____<br>_____ |
| _____<br>_____<br>_____ | _____<br>_____<br>_____ |
| _____<br>_____<br>_____ | _____<br>_____<br>_____ |
| _____<br>_____<br>_____ | _____<br>_____<br>_____ |

For the column on the right, we are going to do something a bit different. What are the aspects of this concept, skill, or practice that can be adapted or scaffolded? For example, if the skill is two-digit subtraction with regrouping, you cannot provide learners with only problems that do NOT require regrouping. The standard clearly says that learners must use regrouping. However, the standard does not say that learners must work alone and without manipulatives or drawings. Thus, we can adapt or scaffold the practice by allowing learners to practice with a thinking partner and/or model the problem with manipulatives or drawings. Therefore, the column on the right shows how we can adapt or scaffold to offer the opportunity for success. Not all learners will need the column on the right, but we must think through these adaptations and scaffolds to support deliberate practice.

Your turn. Return to the table above and generate your list of adaptations or scaffolds that would make deliberate practice more *success oriented*. By the way, there would be distributed scaffolds.

> Take a moment and flip back to examples of distributed scaffolds in Module #10. This may help generate ideas and approaches for adapting and scaffolding deliberate practice.

*Autonomy Supportive.* Deliberate practice opportunities should seek to build learners' sense of ownership in their mathematics learning. Deliberate practice should move us closer to what makes a mathematics learner in our classrooms.

> Flip back to Module #4. What are the characteristics of a mathematics learner that you and your colleagues identified in that module? Transfer that list here.
>
> _____
>
> _____
>
> _____
>
> _____

Learners will be more motivated to engage in deliberate practice if they:

- have a variety of tasks to choose from,

- are able to personalize their practice sessions,

- receive feedback during and after the session,

- have ways to measure their own personal growth,

- are allowed to take risks and try out more difficult tasks, and

- work with peers.

Returning to our four learning experiences or tasks, let's brainstorm ideas for offering autonomy to learners. As before, we modeled one for you.

| CONCEPTS, SKILLS, AND DISPOSITIONS | WAYS TO SUPPORT AUTONOMY |
|---|---|
| *Example: two-digit subtraction with regrouping* | - *Learners are provided with a Tic-Tac-Toe choice board of problems*<br>- *Learners have the option of several different types of manipulatives*<br>- *Learners are asked to develop a story problem that goes with the particular number problem selected* |
| *Example: constructing a mathematical argument* | - *Learners are offered several options of problems with different contexts/ storylines*<br>- *Learners get to decide how to present their argument (e.g., computer, poster paper)*<br>- *Learners can use Loom, Flipgrid, or another technology to present their mathematical argument* |
| _____<br>_____<br>_____ | _____<br>_____<br>_____ |

*(Continued)*

(Continued)

| CONCEPTS, SKILLS, AND DISPOSITIONS | WAYS TO SUPPORT AUTONOMY |
|---|---|
| _____ | _____ |
| _____ | _____ |
| _____ | _____ |
| _____ | _____ |
| _____ | _____ |
| _____ | _____ |
| _____ | _____ |
| _____ | _____ |
| _____ | _____ |
| _____ | _____ |
| _____ | _____ |
| _____ | _____ |

*Developmental Appropriateness.* If we adjust the type of problem from which learners construct an argument, give them choices with manipulatives, offer them a variety of story problems, or allow them to select a way to present their argument, each one of these approaches must still be developmentally appropriate. The mathematics problem must not require mathematics that is too difficult. The rigor of the text in the story problem must be developmentally appropriate.

The chart below shows our four learning experiences or tasks and how we can use the items not included in the blueprint or model to offer a great opportunity for learners to experience success. See if you can brainstorm ideas for increasing experiences of success during deliberate practice sessions by ensuring those sessions are developmentally appropriate. We modeled one for you.

| CONCEPTS, SKILLS, AND DISPOSITIONS | WAYS TO ENSURE DEVELOPMENTAL APPROPRIATENESS |
|---|---|
| *Example: two-digit subtraction with regrouping* | • *Ensure that the number of problems is appropriate and manageable*<br><br>• *Provide different sizes and shapes of manipulatives to ensure learners can manipulate the tools*<br><br>• *Allow learners to type their story problems or dictate them instead of writing them out* |
| *Example: constructing a mathematical argument* | • *Ensure the rigor of the text in the mathematics problems is appropriate for the learner's current reading level*<br><br>• *Ensure the learner knows the strategies for active reading of mathematics problems and can apply them to the text*<br><br>• *Ensure the expectations for the presentation are reasonable for the age and grade level of the learner* |
| _____<br><br>_____<br><br>_____<br><br>_____ | _____<br><br>_____<br><br>_____<br><br>_____ |
| _____<br><br>_____<br><br>_____<br><br>_____ | _____<br><br>_____<br><br>_____<br><br>_____ |

*(Continued)*

(Continued)

| CONCEPTS, SKILLS, AND DISPOSITIONS | WAYS TO ENSURE DEVELOPMENTAL APPROPRIATENESS |
|---|---|
| _____ _____ _____ _____ | _____ _____ _____ _____ |
| _____ _____ _____ _____ | _____ _____ _____ _____ |

Deliberate practice results in the most mathematics learning. Yet deliberate practice—practice that focuses on the conceptual knowledge, procedural fluency, and mathematic practices needing improvement—increases the chances that we will *not* be successful in the beginning. But please hear us out: We are *not* suggesting that with these three approaches to deliberate practices students will *not* experience failure. Plus, we are not in any way insinuating that students should not experience failure. In all learning, especially mathematics, learners will experience a mixture of success and failure as they engage in rigorous concepts, skills, and understandings. But not all failure is bad and not all success is good. Depending on the type of failure and success, we make new or different adjustments to the tasks to increase success, autonomy, and developmental appropriateness.

Wait. Not all failure is bad, and not all success is good. Yes, that is what the research says and what we are unpacking in this final section of the module. Before we do, think for a moment about a time when failure was good and success was bad in mathematics teaching and learning. Describe those situations here.

_____

_____

_____

_____

We will come back to these situations soon.

# PRODUCTIVE FAILURE AND SUCCESS

In our mathematics classrooms, we strive to design and implement tasks and activities with both purposeful and deliberate practice and to eliminate naïve practice. When mathematics learners are engaged in these types of practice, scaffolding ensures the equity of access and opportunity for all our students. If the practice is too challenging and unscaffolded, we are essentially sending a first-time piano player onto the stage with Adele. Scaffolding is designed to provide students with productive success and productive failure experience (Kapur, 2016). Below, find a description of four possible learning events on the left. Connect each one with their conditions on the right. Yes, this is a matching task.

| | |
|---|---|
| 1. Unproductive Failure | A. Unguided problem solving |
| 2. Unproductive Success | B. Structured problem solving |
| 3. Productive Failure | C. Using prior knowledge to figure out a solution followed by more instruction |
| 4. Productive Success | D. Memorizing an algorithm without understanding why |

Of the four conditions, *unproductive failure* yields the smallest gains as students' mathematics thinking is not guided in any way. Learners are just expected to discover what should be learned. You can see how this can negatively influence the development and growth of strategic competence, adaptive reasoning, and productive dispositions. *Unproductive success* is also of limited value as individuals in this condition rely on memorization only but don't ever get to why and how this is applied. There's just no transfer of knowledge, and learners never develop conceptual knowledge, strategic competence, adaptive reasoning, and productive dispositions. Return to the above matching task and make sure you have made these connections in your mathematics classroom.

Now let's move to the beneficial conditions: *productive failure* and *productive success*. Kapur explained that

> The difference between productive failure and productive success is a subtle but an important one. The goal for productive failure is a preparation for learning from subsequent instruction. Thus, it does not matter if students do not achieve successful problem-solving performance initially. In contrast, the goal for productive success is to learn through a successful problem-solving activity itself. (2016, p. 293)

Based on Kapur's model, we identified four possible learning events and their impact (see Figure 11.1). Effective scaffolding requires a mixture of productive failure and productive success. We use productive failure to expose a problem the student didn't know existed and then to follow it with support. Kapur (2019) suggested that "the first job of a teacher isn't to teach. The first job of a teacher is to prepare your students to see, and then to show them."

**FIGURE 11.1** ● Four possible learning events.

| TYPE OF LEARNING EVENT | UNPRODUCTIVE FAILURE | UNPRODUCTIVE SUCCESS | PRODUCTIVE SUCCESS | PRODUCTIVE FAILURE |
|---|---|---|---|---|
| | Unguided problem solving without further instruction | Rote memorization without conceptual understanding | Guided problem solving using prior knowledge and tasks planned for success | Unsuccessful or suboptimal problem-solving using prior knowledge, followed by further instruction |
| **Learning Outcome** | Frustration that leads to abandoning learning | Completion of the task without understanding its purpose or relevance | Consolidation of learning through scaffolded practice | Learning from errors and ensures learners persist in generating and exploring representations and solutions |
| **Useful for** | | | Surface learning of new knowledge firmly anchored to prior knowledge | Deep learning and transfer of knowledge |
| **Undermines** | Agency and motivation | Goal setting and willingness to seek challenge | | |
| **Promotes** | | | Skill development and concept attainment | Use of cognitive, metacognitive, and affective strategies |

Source: Reprinted from Frey, Hattie, and Fisher (2018).

Now, your turn. Think about the standard, unit, or lesson sequence in Modules #2 and #3, respectively. Identify tasks that seem to fit into each of the four categories that Kapur (2016) identified regarding success and failure. Provide some explanation as to why you classified the task the way that you did. Discuss these with your colleagues, and identify which of these tasks might be most effective in facilitating learning.

| UNPRODUCTIVE FAILURE | PRODUCTIVE FAILURE |
|---|---|
| _____ | _____ |
| _____ | _____ |
| _____ | _____ |
| _____ | _____ |

| UNPRODUCTIVE FAILURE | PRODUCTIVE FAILURE |
|---|---|
| _____ | _____ |
| _____ | _____ |
| _____ | _____ |
| _____ | _____ |

## CONCLUSION

Deliberate practice provides students opportunities to experience success and failure, both of which are useful in learning conceptual knowledge, procedural fluency, strategic competence, adaptive reasoning, and productive dispositions. It's when students are engaged in practice that we can apply scaffolds. We also focused on specific aspects of deliberate practice that need careful consideration if the work that we ask students to do is going to be meaningful. These include a success orientation that is supportive of autonomy and developmentally appropriate.

## Exit Ticket

Take a moment and self-evaluate your learning in this module using these statements.

1. I can compare and contrast the different types of practice in my mathematics classroom.

| 1 | 2 | 3 | 4 | 5 |
|---|---|---|---|---|
| Strongly disagree | Disagree | Neutral | Agree | Strongly agree |

Explain the reason for your selection.

_____

_____

*(Continued)*

(Continued)

2. I can explain the differences between productive and unproductive success and failure in my mathematics classroom.

| 1 | 2 | 3 | 4 | 5 |
|---|---|---|---|---|
| Strongly disagree | Disagree | Neutral | Agree | Strongly agree |

Explain the reason for your selection.

_____

_____

3. I can describe the three characteristics of effective deliberate practice in mathematics.

| 1 | 2 | 3 | 4 | 5 |
|---|---|---|---|---|
| Strongly disagree | Disagree | Neutral | Agree | Strongly agree |

Explain the reason for your selection.

_____

_____

4. I can use different techniques to motivate learners to engage in deliberate mathematics practice.

| 1 | 2 | 3 | 4 | 5 |
|---|---|---|---|---|
| Strongly disagree | Disagree | Neutral | Agree | Strongly agree |

Explain the reason for your selection.

_____

_____

# How Do I Generate Evidence of and for Learning in My Classroom?

## MODULE #12

**Learning Intention**

We are learning about the importance of generating evidence in supporting mathematics teaching and learning.

**Success Criteria**

We'll know we've learned this when we can:

1. connect the generation of evidence to scaffolding and practice,

2. identify strategies that generate evidence of learning, and

3. develop sources of evidence that will guide mathematics teaching and learning in our classrooms.

We are not quite done with scaffolding and practice in our mathematics classroom. When we scaffold student learning and engage our learners in deliberate practice, how do we make sure that we have high-quality information about where to go next? How do we know if they really know, understand, and are able to do mathematics? Where are our students in their learning progression of conceptual knowledge, procedural fluency, strategic competence, adaptive reasoning, and productive dispositions? The answer lies in whether teaching and learning in our mathematics classroom are visible. Let's pause for a moment on the idea of teaching and learning being visible.

Consider a recent learning experience in your own mathematics teaching. When the mathematics block ends or the bell rings to end class, **how well can you answer the following questions**?

| | | | |
|---|---|---|---|
| 1. What was the impact of the day's learning experience? | Very Well | Unsure | Not Well |
| 2. Why did you select the particular answer above? | Very Well | Unsure | Not Well |
| 3. Where did your learners experience growth? | Very Well | Unsure | Not Well |
| 4. Why did you select the particular answer above? | Very Well | Unsure | Not Well |
| 5. Where did your learners not experience growth? | Very Well | Unsure | Not Well |
| 6. Why did you select the particular answer above? | Very Well | Unsure | Not Well |
| 7. What are your learners ready for tomorrow? | Very Well | Unsure | Not Well |
| 8. Why did you select the particular answer above? | Very Well | Unsure | Not Well |

To make sense of this previous exercise, let's drop into Renee Nundley's high school algebra class. On the board are the learning intention and success criteria for the day. Her learners are working on linear equations, inequalities, and functions (Standard AI.L).

## LINEAR EQUATIONS, INEQUALITIES, AND FUNCTIONS

| | |
|---|---|
| **AI.L.1** | Represent <u>real-world problems</u> using <u>linear equations</u> and <u>inequalities</u> in <u>one variable</u>, including those with <u>rational number coefficients</u> and <u>variables</u> on <u>both sides of the equal sign</u>. Solve them fluently, explaining the <u>process</u> used and justifying the <u>choice of a solution method.</u> |
| **AI.L.2** | Solve <u>compound linear inequalities</u> in <u>one variable</u>, and represent and <u>solution</u> on a <u>number line</u>. Write a <u>compound linear</u> interpret the <u>inequality given</u> its <u>number line representation</u>. |
| **AI.L.3** | Represent <u>linear functions</u> as <u>graphs from equations</u> (with and without technology), <u>equations</u> from <u>graphs</u>, and <u>equations from tables</u> and other given information(e.g., from a <u>given point</u> on a <u>line</u> and the <u>slope of the line</u>). Find the <u>equation of a line, passing through a given point</u>, that is <u>parallel</u> or <u>perpendicular to a given line</u>. |
| **AI.L.4** | Represent <u>real-world problems</u> that can be modeled with a <u>linear function</u> using <u>equations</u>, <u>graphs</u>, and <u>tables</u>; translate fluently among these <u>representations</u>, and interpret the <u>slope</u> and <u>intercepts</u>. |
| **AI.L.5** | Translate among <u>equivalent forms of equations for linear functions</u>, including <u>slope-intercept</u>, <u>point-slope</u>, and <u>standard</u>. Recognize that <u>different forms</u> reveal more or less information about a given <u>situation</u>. |
| **AI.L.6** | Represent <u>real-world problems</u> using <u>linear inequalities</u> in <u>two variables</u> and solve <u>such problems</u>; interpret the <u>solution set</u> and determine whether it is <u>reasonable</u>. Graph the <u>solutions</u> to a <u>linear inequality</u> in <u>two variables</u> as a <u>half-plane</u>. |
| **AI.L.7** | Solve <u>linear</u> and <u>quadratic equations</u> and <u>formulas</u> for a <u>specified variable</u> to highlight a <u>quantity of interest</u>, using the same <u>reasoning</u> as in solving <u>equations</u>. |

**Source:** Excerpt of the Indiana Department of Education State Standards (2020).

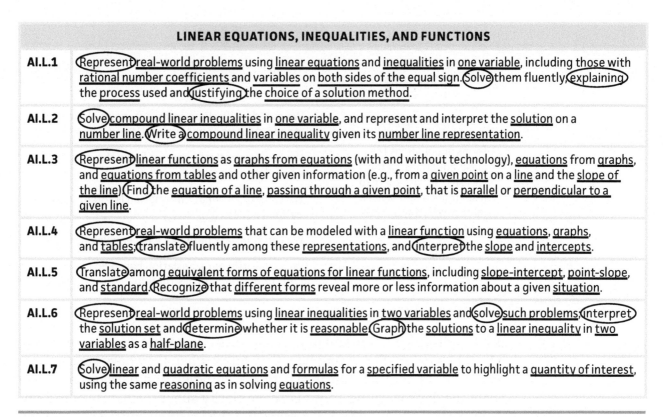

## LINEAR EQUATIONS, INEQUALITIES, AND FUNCTIONS

| | |
|---|---|
| **AI.L.1** | Represent <u>real-world problems</u> using <u>linear equations</u> and <u>inequalities</u> in <u>one variable</u>, including <u>those with rational number coefficients</u> and variables on <u>both sides of the equal sign</u>. Solve them fluently, explaining the <u>process</u> used and justifying the <u>choice of a solution method.</u> |
| **AI.L.2** | Solve <u>compound linear inequalities</u> in <u>one variable</u>, and represent and interpret the <u>solution</u> on a <u>number line</u>. Write a compound linear inequality given its <u>number line representation</u>. |
| **AI.L.3** | Represent <u>linear functions</u> as <u>graphs from equations</u> (with and without technology), <u>equations</u> from <u>graphs</u>, and <u>equations from tables</u> and other given information (e.g., from a <u>given point</u> on a <u>line</u> and the <u>slope of the line</u>). Find the <u>equation of a line, passing through a given point</u>, that is <u>parallel</u> or <u>perpendicular to a given line</u>. |
| **AI.L.4** | Represent <u>real-world problems</u> that can be modeled with a <u>linear function</u> using <u>equations</u>, <u>graphs</u>, and <u>tables</u>; translate fluently among these <u>representations</u>, and interpret the <u>slope</u> and <u>intercepts</u>. |
| **AI.L.5** | Translate among <u>equivalent forms of equations for linear functions</u>, including <u>slope-intercept</u>, <u>point-slope</u>, and <u>standard</u>. Recognize that <u>different forms</u> reveal more or less information about a given <u>situation</u>. |
| **AI.L.6** | Represent <u>real-world problems</u> using <u>linear inequalities</u> in <u>two variables</u> and solve <u>such problems</u>; interpret the <u>solution set</u> and determine whether it is <u>reasonable</u>. Graph the <u>solutions</u> to a <u>linear inequality</u> in <u>two variables</u> as a <u>half-plane</u>. |
| **AI.L.7** | Solve <u>linear</u> and <u>quadratic equations</u> and <u>formulas</u> for a <u>specified variable</u> to highlight a <u>quantity of interest</u>, using the same <u>reasoning</u> as in solving <u>equations</u>. |

**Source:** Excerpt of the Indiana Department of Education State Standards (2020).

| LINEAR EQUATIONS, INEQUALITIES, AND FUNCTIONS | |
|---|---|
| **AI.L.1** | Represent real-world problems using linear equations and inequalities in one variable, including those with rational number coefficients and variables on both sides of the equal sign. Solve them fluently, explaining the process used and justifying the choice of a solution method. |
| **AI.L.2** | Solve compound linear inequalities in one variable, and represent and solution on a number line. Write a compound linear interpret the inequality given its number line representation. |
| **AI.L.3** | Represent linear functions as graphs from equations (with and without technology), equations from graphs, and equations from tables and other given information(e.g., from a given point on a line and the slope of the line). Find the equation of a line, passing through a given point, that is parallel or perpendicular to a given line. |
| **AI.L.4** | Represent real-world problems that can be modeled with a linear function using equations, graphs, and tables; translate fluently among these representations, and interpret the slope and intercepts. |
| **AI.L.5** | Translate among equivalent forms of equations for linear functions, including slope-intercept, point-slope, and standard. Recognize that different forms reveal more or less information about a given situation. |
| **AI.L.6** | Represent real-world problems using linear inequalities in two variables and solve such problems; interpret the solution set and determine whether it is reasonable. Graph the solutions to a linear inequality in two variables as a half-plane. |
| **AI.L.7** | Solve linear and quadratic equations and formulas for a specified variable to highlight a quantity of interest, using the same reasoning as in solving equations. |

**Source:** Excerpt of the Indiana Department of Education State Standards (2020).

| LEARNING INTENTION | SUCCESS CRITERIA |
|---|---|
| We are learning that there are equivalent forms of equations for linear equations, so that we can translate them to learn more about a given mathematical situation. | 1. We can identify slope-intercept, point-slope, and standard forms of linear equations.<br><br>2. We can demonstrate how we know they are equivalent forms.<br><br>3. We can explain what information is communicated by each equation.<br><br>4. We can translate between each equivalent form.<br><br>5. We can justify our translation based on the current mathematical situation. |

Ms. Nundley and her mathematics learners know what they are learning, why they are learning it, and how they know when they have successfully learned it. In addition to the clarity Ms. Nundley and her learners have about the day's learning, they also have clarity about the nature of the evidence necessary to capture the impact of the learning experience and the progress of the learners towards the learning intention.

Take a moment and write the verbs of the success criteria in the left column of the table below:

| VERB | COMPONENT OF MATHEMATICS TEACHING AND LEARNING | WHAT DOES THIS LOOK LIKE? |
|---|---|---|
| _____ _____ | _____ _____ | _____ _____ |
| _____ _____ | _____ _____ | _____ _____ |
| _____ _____ | _____ _____ | _____ _____ |
| _____ _____ | _____ _____ | _____ _____ |
| _____ _____ | _____ _____ | _____ _____ |

We are not done with the success criteria just yet. Based on the verbs you listed in the left column (i.e., identify, demonstrate, explain, translate, and justify), use the middle column to identify the specific element of mathematics teaching and learning represented by the verb. Hint: More than one element can be present in the success criteria. For example, justify may call upon strategic competence and adaptive reasoning.

Finally, take a moment and describe what the verb and element might look like and sound like in your classroom. In other words, if a visitor stopped by your classroom, what would they see and hear? For example, would they hear learners discussing their translations? Would they see students modeling their thinking?

The above table contains the vital information we need in making mathematics teaching and learning visible. The success criteria are the foundation necessary for generating evidence of and for learning. The evidence generated gives us the information we need to increase or fade scaffolds, decide when and where deliberate practice is necessary, and where to go next in mathematics teaching and learning. If the success criteria are what successful learning looks like that day, then we should expect learners to generate evidence throughout the learning experience related to these outcomes.

But this assumes we have designed and implemented learning experiences that offer learners the opportunity to generate such evidence. Consider the following scenarios or possible learning experiences implemented by Ms. Weatherly for these specific learning intentions and success criteria.

*Scenario #1.* Ms. Nundley decides to begin today's class with a quick self-assessment. She provides her learners with the success criteria and, using a Likert scale, asks them to rate their level of comfort with each success criteria. From there, she moves into a mini lesson, during which her learners complete guided notes on the different forms of linear equations. She is always moving around the room to monitor learners as they complete the fill-in notes. In addition to the fill-in notes, she models an example of each form. At the end of the mini lesson, she asks her learners to revisit their self-assessment to see if they feel more comfortable with the success criteria. As a final exit task, learners participate in a Kahoot about the equivalent forms of equations for linear functions.

Using the space provided, write down your thoughts and reactions to this scenario. What is the nature of the evidence captured during the learning experience, and what does the evidence show her and her learners about the progress toward the learning intention?

_____

_____

_____

_____

*Scenario #2.* As the students' file into Ms. Nundley's class, she has a three-minute writing prompt on the board for learners to start as soon as they are settled in their desks. They know that they are to set their timers and work on a response to the writing prompt for three minutes. Today's prompt is an image of a linear function and the statement "Write and explain everything you know about this linear function and its equation." After everyone has had a chance to write for three minutes, she asks her learners to share their responses with their shoulder partners and make any edits to their responses in a different color pen or marker. She moves around the room and listens to their responses. As she moves through the mini lesson, she asks certain students to share their responses to highlight the key points in her mini lesson. At certain spots in the lesson, she pauses and asks learners to summarize their thinking and work through an example with their shoulder partners. But instead of simply filling in facts, the fill-in notes are in the form of questions that they can answer with the help of their shoulder partners. At the end of class, she posts a QR code on the screen that directs learners to an exit ticket on their phones or laptops. The exit ticket takes the following three success criteria and converts them into questions learners must answer.

1. Identify slope-intercept, point-slope, and standard forms of linear equations.

2. Show me an example of how to demonstrate that two equations are equivalent forms of each other.

3. Pick one form of a linear equation and explain what information is communicated by that equation. Be sure to include references to the graph of that equation.

4. Create a mathematical situation that is best described by a specific form of a linear equation. Explain your reasoning.

> Using the space provided, write down your thoughts and reactions to this second scenario. What is the nature of the evidence captured during this learning experience, and what does the evidence show her and her learners about the progress toward the learning intention?
>
> _____
>
> _____
>
> _____
>
> _____

Although there are many similarities and differences between these two possible options for Ms. Nundley's class, we want to direct your attention to the success criteria for both options and the specific strategies selected and implemented in Scenario #2. In both options, the learners were working toward the same success criteria. However, in Scenario #2, learners engaged in strategies that made both Ms. Nundley's teaching and their own thinking visible. Although clarity sets the foundation for the nature of the evidence that must be generated for and of learning, the implementation of the learning experience must actually generate that evidence.

> Okay, pause and process the idea of evidence generation. How would you connect scaffolding, deliberate practice, and evidence generation?
>
> _____
>
> _____
>
> _____
>
> _____

*(Continued)*

(Continued)

As a preview of an upcoming module, how do you think feedback is related to these three ideas?

_____

_____

_____

_____

If we do not generate evidence that is visible during the learning experience, we do not have any insight into students' mathematical thinking, which decisions they make during the learning experience, why they make those decisions, and/or how they are making meaning of the content, skills, and understandings. When we do make teaching and learning visible, we have insight into their conceptual understanding, procedural fluency, strategic competence, adaptive reasoning, or productive dispositions. They also have a better awareness about where they are in the learning progression. Silent mathematics classrooms where learners copy down example after example, lean over the packet of worksheets with pages of mathematics problems, and silently strive to arrive at the right answer is dangerous. The only evidence we have in this dreadful mathematics classroom is evidence of their compliance and stamina! We want more than that from our mathematics learners—you said so yourself in Module #4.

Let's connect a few more dots together with the examples from Ms. Nundley's classroom. First, you can now see that Scenario #2 is the better of the two options for many reasons, not the least of which is developing the types of mathematics learners we described in Module #4. Second, we want to illustrate the relationship between her success criteria, choice of strategies, and the generation of evidence.

In the following chart, you see Ms. Nundley's learning intention and success criteria are listed in the first column. In the second column, list the specific strategy or strategies that provide a source of evidence generated during the learning experience. Do the same for Scenario #2 in the third column.
If you cannot find a source of evidence in one of the options, simply leave the space blank or write "no evidence generated."

You will notice that the learning intention is listed last. This is because the learning intention is the end-goal for the day and should draw on the body of evidence from the entire learning experience.

| LEARNING INTENTION AND SUCCESS CRITERIA | SOURCE OF EVIDENCE | |
|---|---|---|
| **Success Criteria #1:**<br><br>We can identify slope-intercept, point-slope, and standard forms of linear equations. | Scenario #1 | Scenario #2 |
| **Success Criteria #2:**<br><br>We can demonstrate how we know they are equivalent forms. | Scenario #1 | Scenario #2 |
| **Success Criteria #3:**<br><br>We can explain what information is communicated by each equation. | Scenario #1 | Scenario #2 |
| **Success Criteria #4:**<br><br>We can translate between each equivalent form. | Scenario #1 | Scenario #2 |
| **Success Criteria #5:**<br><br>We can justify our translation based on the current mathematical situation. | Scenario #1 | Scenario #2 |
| **Learning Intention:**<br><br>We are learning that there are equivalent forms of equations for linear equations, so that we can translate them to learn more about a given mathematical situation. | Scenario #1 | Scenario #2 |

So, which scenario generated the most evidence for both Ms. Nundley and her students to see their thinking and learning?

In the space below, write the third big idea presented on p. 6 at the start of this Playbook. Yep, simply copy that statement from p. 6 into the area below. This is to emphasize the connections across this Playbook.

_____

_____

_____

_____

Clarity in mathematics teaching and learning, communicated through the learning intentions and success criteria, guide us toward the evidence to generate during the learning experience. The learning intentions and success criteria help us select the strategies, interventions, and tasks that generate that evidence. Deciding which strategies, interventions, and tasks to use in a learning experience can be difficult with so many possible options available to us. The research on what works best in mathematics can lead you down the rabbit hole, never to be heard from again. In fact, there has been some research on this very challenge.

Our guess is that you have a lot coming at you as a teacher. We are pulled in many different directions, and our role as a mathematics teacher comes with other roles and responsibilities. Deciding what strategies to use, which interventions are best for your learners, and what tasks align with the expectations in the standards can be a bit much. Right? We aren't alone in this belief, are we? Do we use a think–pair–share here, or will a forced-choice exit ticket work just as well? Do I have them work problems independently or with a peer? Do we use a Jigsaw in today's learning experience or Reciprocal Teaching? What about a written summary or verbal summary? At the end of the year, aren't they simply going to solve problems?

Posner (2004) looked at the results of having too much to consider in teaching and learning. What happens to us as teachers when we find ourselves in the rabbit hole of research on what works best? He identified the following three common outcomes:

1. We disregard the research and simply go with our gut. This approach leads us to often teach mathematics just as we were taught mathematics. In this situation, mathematics learning is solely by chance—the chance that our learners approach mathematics the same way we do or did.

2. We might pick those strategies, interventions, and tasks that we like or those with which we are most comfortable. Again, we leave learning to chance.

3. We also might simply gather or borrow lots of different strategies, interventions, or tasks and create a toolkit. Then, we simply start "throwing spaghetti against the wall to see what sticks." This is also leaving learning to chance—the chance I might pick a strategy, intervention, or task that aligns with the success criteria.

To ensure that conceptual knowledge, procedural fluency, strategic competence, adaptive reasoning, and productive dispositions grow and develop by design, we must generate visible evidence to see it happening, to see our impact on student learning. Remember those questions at the start of this module. Flip back there now and review them carefully. Whether you could circle Very Well instead of Not Well is singularly correlated with the amount of evidence generated in your mathematics classroom. Let's solidify this in our own learning.

> The success of my teaching and my students' learning in mathematics depends on making teaching and learning visible.

Let's return one more time to Ms. Nundley's learning intention and success criteria. On p. 186 locate the verbs used in her success criteria one more time. Then, write those verbs in the space below.

_____

_____

The verbs of the success criteria clarify and specify the evidence we and our learners need to generate during the mathematics learning experience. What's important to emphasize here is that those verbs must be rooted in the standards we analyzed in Modules #2 and #3. These five verbs point us in the direction of certain strategies, interventions, and tasks. At the same time, they help us stay away from others. For example, if Ms. Nundley needs her learners to be able to explain what information is communicated by each equation, then she needs to look for and select a strategy, intervention, or task that gives them the opportunity to practice explaining. And if everyone is not yet ready to explain, she needs to select a strategy, intervention, or task that allows her to scaffold explaining.

Below are several choices available to Ms. Nundley. Based on the verb *explain*, **circle** the ones that give learners the opportunity to practice explaining and can be scaffolded for learners so that they can explain at the highest level possible.

*We can explain what information is communicated by each equation.*

1. A Kahoot or some other clicker-based task

2. Think–Pair–Share

3. Guided Notes

4. Forced-Choice Check for Understanding

5. Thumbs Up, Thumbs Down Review

6. Three-Minute Write

Hopefully you selected options 2 and 6. A think–pair–share and a three-minute write provide an opportunity for learners to explain. A think–pair–share is a verbal opportunity, and a three-minute write is a written opportunity. But this does not mean there is anything wrong with the other four options. They are just not going to give us evidence for this specific success criteria.

Consider Ms. Weatherly's first success criteria:

*We can identify slope-intercept, point-slope, and standard forms of linear equations.*

Now which options provide the evidence needed? ALL OF THEM! The difference lies not in the strategy, intervention, or task but in the purpose for which we use it in the learning experience.

Let's apply this to the learning intentions and success criteria you might use in your daily mathematics teaching and learning. Consider the work you have been doing with Modules #2 and #3. You have now noticed that this foundational work analyzing standards and developing a learning progression is the anchor for everything else in this Playbook.

The chart that follows should look very familiar to you. Develop a daily learning intention and set of success criteria. Then, list out specific strategies that would generate the evidence needed to answer those key questions at the start of this module. They are provided here for your convenience.

1. What was the impact of the day's learning experience?

2. Where did my learners experience growth?

3. Where did my learners not experience growth?

List as many as you can for now. Then, when it is time to implement them into your mathematics teaching, you can select those that are most engaging for your learners.

| LEARNING INTENTIONS | EXAMPLES OF SUCCESS CRITERIA | STRATEGIES FOR GENERATING EVIDENCE |
|---|---|---|
| _____ | _____ | _____ |
| _____ | _____ | _____ |
| _____ | _____ | _____ |
| _____ | _____ | _____ |

| LEARNING INTENTIONS | EXAMPLES OF SUCCESS CRITERIA | STRATEGIES FOR GENERATING EVIDENCE |
|---|---|---|
| _____ | _____ | _____ |
| _____ | _____ | _____ |
| _____ | _____ | _____ |
| _____ | _____ | _____ |
| _____ | _____ | _____ |
| _____ | _____ | _____ |
| _____ | _____ | _____ |
| _____ | _____ | _____ |
| _____ | _____ | _____ |
| _____ | _____ | _____ |
| _____ | _____ | _____ |
| _____ | _____ | _____ |

One incredibly powerful finding about what works best in mathematics teaching and learning is that the potential impact of strategies lies in how visible they make student thinking and learning. Put another way, those evidence-based practices that have the highest potential impact on learning all make student thinking and learning visible. For example, which teaching and learning strategy do you think has the highest effect size: lecturing or classroom discussion?

The answer is classroom discussion, by far. The reason for this striking difference (Lectures = –0.26; Classroom Discussion = 0.82) lies in the fact that one of these approaches provides visible evidence to both us and our students. This evidence allows us to see conceptual knowledge, procedural fluency, strategic competence, adaptive reasoning, and productive dispositions!

This is powerful. This is a key element of the Mathematics Playbook.

Try applying this finding to other strategies. Figure 12.1 is a list of strategies. Use the chart to test out the finding that the most effective teaching and learning strategies make thinking and learning visible.

**FIGURE 12.1** ● Analyzing effective teaching and learning strategies.

| STRATEGY | DOES IT GENERATE VISIBLE EVIDENCE? | EFFECT SIZE FROM www.visible learning metax.com | WHY? WHAT POTENTIAL EVIDENCE IS GENERATED? |
|---|---|---|---|
| Concept Mapping | Yes or No | | |
| Clickers | Yes or No | | |
| Strategy Monitoring | Yes or No | | |
| Teaching Test-Taking | Yes or No | | |
| Outlining and Summarizing | Yes or No | | |

| STRATEGY | DOES IT GENERATE VISIBLE EVIDENCE? | EFFECT SIZE FROM www.visible learning metax.com | WHY? WHAT POTENTIAL EVIDENCE IS GENERATED? |
|---|---|---|---|
| Mathematics Problem Solving | Yes or No | | |
| Cooperative Learning | Yes or No | | |
| Worked Examples | Yes or No | | |
| One-to-One Laptops | Yes or No | | |
| Manipulatives | Yes or No | | |
| Programmed Instruction | Yes or No | | |

Do you see the point? Evidence-generating strategies matter. One-to-one laptops aren't a bad thing. The question is, however, how are we using them to generate evidence? High-impact strategies are important because they make thinking and learning visible. They give us evidence about conceptual knowledge, procedural fluency, strategic competence, adaptive reasoning, and productive dispositions, evidence about where to go next.

To support your learning journey, we want to provide you with a template to facilitate discussions regarding evidence generation (Figure 12.2). This work should be part of our planning and professional learning community (PLC+) work with our grade-level teams or content-level groups.

**FIGURE 12.2** ● Evidence generation template.

| LEARNING INTENTION AND SUCCESS CRITERIA | SOURCE OF EVIDENCE |
|---|---|
|  |  |
|  |  |
|  |  |
|  |  |

# Exit Ticket

Take a moment and self-evaluate your learning in this module using these statements.

1. I can connect the generation of evidence to scaffolding and practice.

| 1 | 2 | 3 | 4 | 5 |
|---|---|---|---|---|
| Strongly disagree | Disagree | Neutral | Agree | Strongly agree |

Explain the reason for your selection.

_____

_____

2. I can identify strategies that generate evidence of learning.

| 1 | 2 | 3 | 4 | 5 |
|---|---|---|---|---|
| Strongly disagree | Disagree | Neutral | Agree | Strongly agree |

Explain the reason for your selection.

_____

_____

3. I can develop sources of evidence that will guide mathematics teaching and learning in our classrooms.

| 1 | 2 | 3 | 4 | 5 |
|---|---|---|---|---|
| Strongly disagree | Disagree | Neutral | Agree | Strongly agree |

Explain the reason for your selection.

_____

_____

# MODULE 13

# How Do I Notice the Evidence in My Classroom?

## MODULE #13

**Learning Intention**

We are now learning about the practice of noticing and how noticing supports mathematics teaching and learning in my classroom.

**Success Criteria**

We'll know we've learned this when we can:

1. define what is meant by teacher noticing and student noticing,

2. describe how teacher noticing and student noticing supports all elements of mathematics learning, and

3. intentionally plan for noticing in our mathematics teaching and our students' learning.

This module is all about what we notice in our mathematics classrooms. If we are going to generate evidence in our classroom about our mathematics learners, we have to do something with that evidence; that evidence must be useful; that evidence must help our learners and

us decide (fill in the blanks) _____ to go
_____. Otherwise, we are data rich and information poor. Otherwise, the evidence gathering is both busy work for us and for our learners. This module, alongside the next module, answers the question "Now what?" What do we do with the evidence generated throughout the learning experience? The answers are (a) notice it, and (b) use it to give, receive, and integrate feedback into mathematics teaching and learning.

Let's address what is meant by noticing. We will save feedback for Module #14.

---

Flip back to the beginning of Module #12 on pp. 183–184. We presented three questions to consider about students' mathematics learning. Write those three questions here:

1. _____

2. _____

3. _____

---

As you know, our capacity for answering these three questions comes from the existence of visible evidence. The reliability and validity of those answers comes from our capacity to notice.

---

What do you think is meant by noticing, specifically, teacher noticing? Use the space below to jot down your thinking.

_____

_____

_____

_____

---

Starting with the basics, noticing is an active process that involves multiple systems in our bodies. This is often referred to as *attention* and *perception*. When you first look at an image, you initially notice certain characteristics or features. After viewing the picture for some time, you notice other characteristics, and then some characteristics you only notice **after someone points them out to you.**

Use the space below to brainstorm some factors that influence what you initially notice, notice after some time, or never notice without the help of others.

_____

_____

_____

_____

You may also have identified influences like prior knowledge, prior experiences, personal interests, and the context. For example, if you are very familiar with the common misconceptions associated with a particular concept or skill (prior knowledge), that will influence what you notice in these images. If you have taught the same grade level or level of mathematics for some time (prior experiences), that will influence what you notice in the generated evidence. If solving word problems, simplifying rational expressions, or geometric proofs are your jam (personal interests), you will notice different things in student evidence. Finally, and most importantly, if you view the evidence alongside the learning intentions, success criteria, the learning progression, and analyzed standard (context), that may play a role in what you notice as well.

However, the very things that help us notice better can also cause us problems. Take a look at the list of phrases below and see if any of them sound familiar to you:

- I don't understand why they are not getting this. This is pretty basic.

- Oh, I know they know this. They must have been distracted.

- The answer is obvious. I am surprised that they struggled to solve this problem.

- I am not sure how to make this any clearer.

- They are not seeing that this problem is just like the other problem.

- They always struggle with this concept.

Let's be honest. We have all muttered these statements at some point in our careers. And, if we won't admit it out loud, we can at least agree that we have heard colleagues make these statements.

These statements reflect biases in our noticing. Psychologists have studied the biases in our thinking for a very long time and have accumulated a list of cognitive biases that can trip us up (Kahneman, 2011; Korteling & Toet, 2022). As mathematics teachers, we are not immune to these cognitive biases. In fact, we may be at an even greater risk than others.

Although many, many cognitive biases exist (some psychologists estimate there to be as many as 175), we want to highlight a few specific ones because they can negatively influence our noticing of evidence in our mathematics classroom.

Using any internet search engine, dig up information on the following cognitive biases. Summarize your findings in the table.

| COGNITIVE BIAS | SUMMARY | HOW DOES THE COGNITIVE BIAS AFFECT MY NOTICING? |
|---|---|---|
| Bizarreness Effect | | |
| Negativity Bias | | |
| Anchoring Bias | | |
| Framing Effect | | |
| Confirmation Bias | | |

| COGNITIVE BIAS | SUMMARY | HOW DOES THE COGNITIVE BIAS AFFECT MY NOTICING? |
|---|---|---|
| Selective Perception | | |
| Hot Hand Fallacy | | |
| Stereotyping | | |
| Curse of Knowledge | | |

These biases are quite interesting, aren't they? Have you found yourself subject to these biases? If a learner uses a bizarre approach to solving a problem, do we respond differently to that learner than to one who uses our approach to the problem? If a learner frames something well, do we overlook a mistake? Do we notice things differently with learners that are labeled as "strong in mathematics"? Do we forget what it was like starting out in mathematics and are cursed by our own knowledge?

To be clear, these biases are unavoidable and a natural part of being human. Falling into these biases while noticing the evidence generated in our classrooms does not make us a bad teacher. Awareness of these biases helps us to be an AMAZING mathematics teacher because we have a much higher chance of truly noticing the evidence in front of us.

So, what really is noticing?

# NOTICING

In our schools and classrooms, *noticing* is the active process of attending to what is happening during a learning experience: the interactions or tasks, interpreting what we see, and then using that interpretation to decide where to go next (Schoenfeld, 2011).

| Attend to the evidence generated from our mathematics strategies, interventions, and tasks. | → | Interpret the evidence using learning intentions, success criteria, the learning progression, and analyzed standard. | → | Integrate that interpretation and meaning into where to go next in mathematics teaching and learning. |

This concept of noticing applies to both teachers and learners. When we are engaged in noticing, we often engage in an internal dialogue about what is going on in our classroom.

| NOTICING BY THE TEACHER . . . | NOTICING BY THE STUDENT . . . |
|---|---|
| What am I noticing about my learners as they engage in the learning experience? | What am I noticing about myself as I engage in the learning experience? |
| What are my students noticing as they engage in their learning experience? | What are my peers noticing as they engage with me in the learning experience? |
| What does this tell me about their current progress toward the learning intention and success criteria? | What does this tell me about my current progress toward the learning intention and success criteria? |

**Source:** Adapted from Sherin et al. (2011).

What we want to notice and what we want our students to notice is communicated through our directions, gestures, body language, posters on the wall, models or objects on the demonstration table, the arrangement of the classroom, and our learning intentions and success criteria. Scaffolding and deliberate practice requires learners and us to engage in successful **noticing** of the evidence generated during a strategy, intervention, or task. And as we will see in the next module, teacher noticing and student noticing is required to identify where that feedback should be given, received, and integrated.

We want to take an extra step in linking this aspect of the Playbook with the foundational work in Modules #1 through #4. One role of standards, analyzing standards, developing learning progressions, and articulating what it means to be a mathematics learner is that these foundational pieces provide the lenses needed to notice where learners are making progress or not making progress toward the intended outcomes. We have the lenses needed to notice when and who our teaching is benefiting and when and who our teaching is not benefiting.

On the flip side, when our learners are clear on the three questions of clarity (write those three questions below from p. 194 in Module #12),

1. _____,

2. _____, and

3. _____.

they have the lenses needed to notice their current level of understanding, where they are making progress, and where they needed additional learning. They have the lenses needed to frame their strategic competence, adaptive reasoning, and adaptive dispositions. We can develop noticing skills by preplanning what we are looking for during the learning experience and anticipating student responses. That's what we want to explore next.

Eli Revia is planning his unit on surface area and volume. His tenth-grade team has devoted a significant amount of time analyzing the standard and has now developed a learning progression, identifying the major success criteria for the first part of this unit focusing on Trigonometry and the Unit Circle, specifically, on the concept of a radian measure (see Figure 13.1).

**FIGURE 13.1** ● Georgia Standards—Geometric and spatial reasoning.

| GEOMETRIC & SPATIAL REASONING – TRIGONOMETRY AND THE UNIT CIRCLE | | |
|---|---|---|
| **G.GSR.7: EXPLORE THE CONCEPT OF A RADIAN MEASURE AND SPECIAL RIGHT TRIANGLES.** | | |
| | **EXPECTATIONS** | **EXPECTATIONS EVIDENCE OF STUDENT LEARNING** |
| G.GSR.7.1 | Explore and interpret a radian as the ratio of the arc length to the radius of a circle. | **Strategies and Methods**<br>• Students should be given opportunities to make sense of the meaning of radians conceptually through exploration with visual tools.<br>• Using hands on tools and technology visualizations, students should have opportunities to **explore** and **develop** an understanding of the relationship between the radius of a circle, an arc length, and the associated radian measure. |

*(Continued)*

(Continued)

| GEOMETRIC & SPATIAL REASONING – TRIGONOMETRY AND THE UNIT CIRCLE | | |
|---|---|---|
| **G.GSR.7: EXPLORE THE CONCEPT OF A <u>RADIAN MEASURE</u> AND <u>SPECIAL RIGHT TRIANGLES</u>.** | | |
| | **EXPECTATIONS** | **EXPECTATIONS EVIDENCE OF STUDENT LEARNING** |
| G.GSR.7.2 | (Explore) and (explain) the relationship between radian measures and degree measures and (convert fluently) between degree and radian measures. | **Fundamentals** <br><br> • Students should be able to (convert) **fluently** (flexibly, accurately, and efficiently) between <u>degree</u> and <u>radian</u> <u>measures</u> to (solve) <u>real-life</u> <u>problems</u>. <br><br> **Strategies and Methods** <br><br> • Students should have opportunities to (explore) and (discover) experimentally the relationship between <u>radian measure</u> and <u>degree</u> <u>measure</u> (using) <u>visual tools</u>. |
| G.GSR.7.3 | (Use) special right triangles <u>on the unit circle</u> to (determine the values) of sine, cosine, and tangent for $30° \left(\frac{\pi}{6}\right)$, $45° \left(\frac{\pi}{4}\right)$ and $60° \left(\frac{\pi}{3}\right)$ angle measures. (Use) reflections of triangles to (determine) reference angles and (identify) coordinate values in all four quadrants of the coordinate plane. | **Fundamentals** <br><br> • Students should be able to (articulate) the pattern associated with angle measures in all <u>four quadrants</u> of the unit circle, e.g., $\overline{150°}$ as 180°–30°, $\overline{210°}$ as 180°+30°, 330° as 360°–30°, etc. <br><br> • Students should (explore), (interpret), and (use) radian measures based on <u>conversions from degree measures</u>, such as 150°, 210°, etc., and (articulate) the <u>patterns</u> associated with those radian measures, including the connection of $5\pi\, 6 \approx 2.617$ <u>radius units</u> measured <u>along the arc length</u> of the circle. <br><br> • Through explorations, students (develop an understanding) that a <u>unit circle</u> has a <u>radius</u> equal to 1. <br><br> • This learning objective is limited to angle measures of $30° \left(\frac{\pi}{6}\right)$, $45° \left(\frac{\pi}{4}\right)$ and $60° \left(\frac{\pi}{3}\right)$, and their <u>associated reflected</u> <u>angles</u> within one counterclockwise <u>revolution</u> of the unit circle. | |

**Source:** Georgia Department of Education, 2021.

To solve problems involving radian measures using the unit circle, students must be able to:

1. Identify the arc length on a circle.

2. Identify the radius of a circle.

3. Find the arc length and radius of the circle.

4. Calculate the ratio of the arc length to the radius of a circle.

5. Explain what a radian is.

6. Use technology to model a radian.

7. Explain the relationship between arc length, radius, and radian.

8. Interpret a radian measure for a given circle.

Prior to implementing any learning experience during this unit, Mr. Revia develops a list of evidence that must be generated during the learning experiences associated with this part of the standard and unit. From there, he develops a list of look-fors, things he is going to watch for and listen for during the learning experiences. Several items on this list are areas that often challenge learners. Let's look at Mr. Revia's success criteria for one learning intention.

| LEARNING INTENTIONS | EXAMPLES OF SUCCESS CRITERIA | WHAT WOULD YOU BE LOOKING FOR? | |
|---|---|---|---|
| **GEOMETRIC & SPATIAL REASONING: TRIGONOMETRY AND THE UNIT CIRCLE (EXPLORE THE CONCEPT OF A RADIAN MEASURE AND SPECIAL RIGHT TRIANGLES.)** | | | |
| **Learning Intention:**<br><br>I am learning about the special relationships on a circle so that I can understand what is meant by a radian. | I can locate the radius of a circle.<br><br>I can interpret a model to show how the arc length and the radius are associated with radian measure.<br><br>I can explain the relationship between the radius of a circle and the arc length of a circle.<br><br>I can summarize what a radian is using a circle. | Look-fors<br><br>• Do they use the mathematical vocabulary when talking about the radius, the arc length, and a radian?<br><br>• Do they use tools to model their thinking?<br><br>• Can they ask and answer questions like, "what do you think will happen next?", "why do you think so?"<br><br>• Do they use their experiences from the task to generate their summary? | Possible Challenges<br><br>• My learners may need a front-end scaffold for the mathematical vocabulary.<br><br>• They often back up their predictions with their life experiences and not evidence from their models; may need distributed scaffold of a model or exemplary model.<br><br>• They often ask fact-based questions and do not focus on why or how questions; may need distributed scaffolding of question examples or question stems. |

By engaging in this brainstorm session, Mr. Revia is better prepared to notice the relevant aspects of the learning experience and less likely to get distracted or miss a key concept, skill, or understanding. Furthermore, the preplanning work helps to lessen the probability that cognitive biases derail the use of evidence generated during the learning experience. Likewise, his learners are less likely to attend to irrelevant details or miss a key concept, skill, or understanding.

Let's return to the examples of learning intentions and success criteria from earlier in the module. As you revisit these learning intentions and success criteria, if you were the classroom teacher, what would you be looking for during the learning experience?

| LEARNING INTENTIONS | EXAMPLES OF SUCCESS CRITERIA | WHAT WOULD YOU BE LOOKING FOR? | |
|---|---|---|---|
| **Learning Intention:**<br><br>We are learning that there are equivalent forms of equations for linear equations, so that we can translate them to learn more about a given mathematical situation. | **Success Criteria:**<br><br>We can identify slope-intercept, point-slope, and standard forms of linear equations.<br><br>We can demonstrate how we know they are equivalent forms.<br><br>We can explain what information is communicated by each equation.<br><br>We can translate between each equivalent form.<br><br>We can justify our translation based on the current mathematical situation. | **Look-fors** | **Possible Challenges** |

To close out this module, we want to give you another chance to connect analyzing the standard, learning progressions, learning intentions, success criteria, evidence generation, and noticing to your mathematics teaching and learning.

Grab those valuable documents and that incredible work from Modules #2 and #3. Again, we have used this work throughout the entire Playbook. For now, take the learning intentions and success criteria developed in the previous module and preplan the source of evidence and the look-fors that will help you be a better noticer and avoid, to the best of your ability, cognitive biases.

| LEARNING INTENTION AND SUCCESS CRITERIA | SOURCE OF EVIDENCE | WHAT ARE YOU LOOKING FOR IN THIS EVIDENCE? |
|---|---|---|
| | 1. | |
| | 2. | |
| | 3. | |
| | 4. | |
| | | |
| | | |

To continue to support your learning journey, we want to provide you with a template (Figure 13.2) to facilitate discussions around noticing. This work should go along with the other work in this Playbook as part of our planning and professional learning community (PLC+) work with our grade-level teams or content-level groups.

**FIGURE 13.2** ● Noticing template.

| LEARNING INTENTION AND SUCCESS CRITERIA | SOURCE OF EVIDENCE | WHAT ARE YOU LOOKING FOR IN THIS EVIDENCE? |
|---|---|---|
| | | |
| | | |
| | | |
| | | |

online resources ♗ This resource is available for download at **resources.corwin.com/themathematicsplaybook**.

Take a deep breath. You have done great work! We are approaching the final modules in the Playbook. Once we have generated evidence and engaged in noticing, we now must use our noticing's to give, receive, and integrate feedback into where we go next. Just noticing makes us a passive observer of mathematics teaching and learning. Noticing and acting on that noticing makes us active mathematics teachers that amplify our impact on conceptual knowledge, procedural fluency, strategic competence, adaptive reasoning, and productive dispositions.

## Exit Ticket

Take a moment and self-evaluate your own learning in this module using these statements.

1. I can define what is meant by teacher noticing and student noticing.

| 1 | 2 | 3 | 4 | 5 |
|---|---|---|---|---|
| Strongly disagree | Disagree | Neutral | Agree | Strongly agree |

Explain the reason for your selection.

_____

_____

2. I can describe how teacher noticing and student noticing supports all elements of mathematics learning.

| 1 | 2 | 3 | 4 | 5 |
|---|---|---|---|---|
| Strongly disagree | Disagree | Neutral | Agree | Strongly agree |

Explain the reason for your selection.

_____

_____

3. I can intentionally plan for noticing in our mathematics teaching and our students' learning.

| 1 | 2 | 3 | 4 | 5 |
|---|---|---|---|---|
| Strongly disagree | Disagree | Neutral | Agree | Strongly agree |

Explain the reason for your selection.

_____

_____

# MODULE 14

# What Is the Role of Feedback in My Classroom?

## MODULE #14

**Learning Intention**

We are learning about feedback so that we can incorporate it into our daily practice to scaffold and assess student's progress toward mastery.

**Success Criteria**

We'll know we've learned this when we can:

1. identify the foundational components of feedback,

2. describe the three levels of feedback, and

3. explain why it is important to respond to feedback and provide examples.

# COMPARE AND CONTRAST

Go back to Module #10 to review how to scaffold tasks in the mathematical classroom. Then complete the Venn diagram below. What is the relationship between scaffolding, feedback, and assessment?

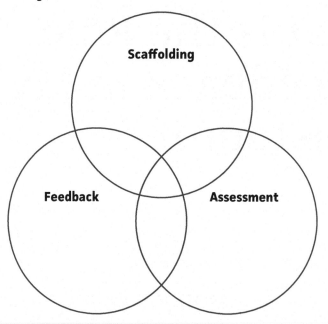

We learned in Module #10 that scaffolding engages and supports students through productive struggle and that feedback can serve a similar function. Feedback is the information that tells us how we are doing in our efforts to reach a goal (Wiggins, 2012). It is not uncommon to see feedback as going in one direction, with teachers *giving* it to students. Feedback has an overall effect size of 0.54 (Hattie, 2023), so for it to be effective, it must also be *received*. If we think about it from a different angle, the giver and receiver mutually trust and respect each other such that feedback is used to bridge the learning gap between their current level of knowledge and where we want it to be.

Think about the last mathematics lesson you implemented. When they were engaged with a learning experience or task, what instructional techniques did you use to elicit their feedback about their learning process? How did you know whether your response was well received? Jot these thoughts down in the space below so that we can revisit them throughout our work in this Playbook.

_____

_____

_____

_____

# THE FOUNDATION FOR FEEDBACK

Effective educators in mathematics know that their learners need more than access to experts in curriculum and instruction. They also need to believe that they are a part of a classroom culture that places just as much importance on building and maintaining relationships with the teacher and their peers. The likelihood that it will be well received can be predicted by how well *students* believe that the teacher attends to them (Almarode et al., 2023):

- **Care:** A learning atmosphere with trust and respect. When care is not established and maintained, students are guarded and unwilling to communicate what they do not understand so they do not accept feedback or use it as an opportunity to grow.

- **Credibility:** The belief that an individual is worthy of listening to and learning from. When students believe that the teacher is competent, then their feedback will be better received.

- **Clarity:** An understanding of what is being learned, why we are learning it, and how we will know when we have learned it. Students interpret them as goals and view feedback as a valuable means to meet each one.

- **Communication:** The way in which a message is sent and the ability to discern whether the recipient can interpret and act on it as intended.

The *who*, *what*, and *how* of feedback are built on a foundation of the four components above (Almarode et al., 2023):

- **Who** is giving, receiving, and integration feedback depends on *care* and *credibility*.

- **What** feedback is given, received, and integrated depends on *clarity*.

- **How** the feedback is given depends on *communication*.

## SELF-ASSESSMENT (PART I)

Let's pause to check in with ourselves. Use the rating scales below to assess yourself in the four domains discussed above.

I believe I demonstrate . . .

*(Continued)*

(Continued)

1) Care

| 1 | 2 | 3 | 4 | 5 |
|---|---|---|---|---|
| Strongly disagree | Disagree | Neutral | Agree | Strongly agree |

2) Credibility

| 1 | 2 | 3 | 4 | 5 |
|---|---|---|---|---|
| Strongly disagree | Disagree | Neutral | Agree | Strongly agree |

3) Clarity

| 1 | 2 | 3 | 4 | 5 |
|---|---|---|---|---|
| Strongly disagree | Disagree | Neutral | Agree | Strongly agree |

4) Communication

| 1 | 2 | 3 | 4 | 5 |
|---|---|---|---|---|
| Strongly disagree | Disagree | Neutral | Agree | Strongly agree |

## SELF-ASSESSMENT (PART II)

Now complete the assessment again, but this time predict how your students might respond. Are they similar or different?

My students believe that I demonstrate

1) Care

| 1 | 2 | 3 | 4 | 5 |
|---|---|---|---|---|
| Strongly disagree | Disagree | Neutral | Agree | Strongly agree |

2) Credibility

| 1 | 2 | 3 | 4 | 5 |
|---|---|---|---|---|
| Strongly disagree | Disagree | Neutral | Agree | Strongly agree |

3) Clarity

| 1 | 2 | 3 | 4 | 5 |
|---|---|---|---|---|
| Strongly disagree | Disagree | Neutral | Agree | Strongly agree |

4) Communication

| 1 | 2 | 3 | 4 | 5 |
|---|---|---|---|---|
| Strongly disagree | Disagree | Neutral | Agree | Strongly agree |

# ELEMENTS OF FEEDBACK

Almarode et al. (2023) described three aspects of feedback: giving, receiving, and adjusting. Note that until this point, we described the giver as the teacher and the receiver as the student. However, the giver may be the teacher or the student, and the same is true of the receiver. Earlier we noted that giving feedback isn't enough because it must also be received. We argue that if the receiver does not use it to adjust (assuming that course correction is needed), then it falls short of its intended purpose.

Feedback is mediated by the relationship between the giver and the receiver, and receivers may judge how useful they believe the feedback to be. The three types of feedback are about the task, the process used in the task, and the self-regulation needed to drive learning (Hattie, 2023). Figure 14.1 contains examples of each.

**FIGURE 14.1** ● Three levels of feedback.

| TASK LEVEL | PROCESS LEVEL | SELF-REGULATION LEVEL |
|---|---|---|
| • The most common type of feedback<br>• Builds surface-level knowledge<br>• Known as "corrective feedback" because it tells students if they are right or wrong<br>• Not generalizable to learning because it is specific to the task<br>• More limited impact on future student learning, but useful when building surface-level knowledge | • Aimed at cognitive and metacognitive processes used to create the product or complete a task<br>• Fosters understanding of the relationship between concepts (deep learning)<br>• Reinforces learning strategies or provides clues to develop different ones<br>• Error detection approaches to learn from mistakes<br>• Impacts future learning situations because students can apply it to novel situations | • Builds student skills in monitoring their own learning processes<br>• Provides greater confidence to continue engaging with the task<br>• The student is willing to invest in and seek feedback<br>• Impacts future learning situations when used to forward learning (not as a comment on their character) |

*(Continued)*

(Continued)

| TEACHER-TO-STUDENT EXAMPLES | TEACHER-TO-STUDENT EXAMPLES | TEACHER-TO-STUDENT EXAMPLES |
|---|---|---|
| • "You didn't cite your sources in the second paragraph. Add those sources to strengthen your claim."<br><br>• "You haven't met the success criteria yet because . . ."<br><br>• "Let's look at the exemplar and discuss the differences between it and your work." | • "What was the approach you used to solve this problem?"<br><br>• "Are there other ways to verify your answer?"<br><br>• "How can you take what you learned here and apply it to other situations?" | • "How do you know that you're on the right track?"<br><br>• "How could you strengthen this project so that you are achieving the success criteria?"<br><br>• "What did you learn about yourself as a learner that you didn't realize before?" |
| **STUDENT-TO-TEACHER EXAMPLES** | **STUDENT-TO-TEACHER EXAMPLES** | **STUDENT-TO-TEACHER EXAMPLES** |
| • "I don't understand what I'm supposed to do next."<br><br>• "Did I do this right?" | • "Like this?"<br><br>• "Isn't there an easier way to do this? Why do I have to do it this way?" | • "This is too hard. I give up."<br><br>• "I'm too dumb. I'm not good at ____." |

**Source:** Reprinted from Frey et al. (2023).

## RESPONDING TO FEEDBACK

The feedback process gives us insight into the effectiveness of our mathematical teaching practice and how students are or are not moving through the mathematical learning process. We do this by listening and posing questions to check for understanding (revisit Module #10's Figure 10.3 for types of questions). The overall effect size for feedback is notable on its own (0.54), but when we pair it with a response, then its impact on student achievement increases. In case some doubt might still be lingering about this as an instructional strategy, we will look to the global research database on visiblelearningmetax.com:

- Feedback aimed more at improving the content, facts, or ideas has an effect size of 0.63.

- The timing of feedback has an effect size of 0.89.

- When feedback is given with cues to advance to next steps in learning, then the effect size is 1.01.

Throughout the module, you may have noticed how feedback overlaps with scaffolding and assessment processes. The reality is that they have an interconnected relationship because they are essential to effective mathematical instruction.

Let's take a processing pause to reflect on our practice "in the moment." While students are working on a task, how do you respond to students when they are meeting the learning intention and success criteria? When you discover a learning gap, what is your approach to redirect them?

_____

_____

_____

_____

When students show us where they are on the intended learning roadmap, we should respond with appreciation and coaching feedback. Appreciative feedback recognizes and rewards learners for the great work that they have accomplished, and coaching feedback expands their knowledge, skills, and capacities (Vrabie, 2021). When incorporated into practice, we have an opportunity to address feelings, strengthen relationships, and support students' intrinsic motivation (Vrabie, 2021). When we discover that students need redirection, we can use prompts and cues as we do in distributive scaffolding (see Module #10). If errors or misconceptions persist, then teachers can directly reteach, model, or give the answer. Although this is not our initial response, we must bring closure to the learning and ensure that students don't leave the experience without it being a successful one.

This is a great time to revisit Module #10. In the space below, what are three key takeaways about prompts? What are three important things to remember about cues?

Three key takeaways about prompts are:

1. _____

2. _____

3. _____

Three important things to remember about cues are . . .

1. _____

2. _____

3. _____

## PLANNING FOR FEEDBACK

When we plan a lesson with rigorous mathematical tasks, we understand the value of productive struggle and why we strategically embed scaffolds throughout its design. Similarly, we consider opportunities where we gather feedback to assess their progress, anticipate common errors and misconceptions, and consider how we might respond to them. Let's apply what we learned in this module to an upcoming lesson using the guiding prompts and questions in the table.

| | | | |
|---|---|---|---|
| **Step 1)** Choose an upcoming, standards-based mathematical task. | | | |
| **Step 2)** What are the learning intentions and success criteria aligned to the task? | | | |
| **Step 3)** What observations might you see or hear that indicates a progression <u>toward</u> mastery? How will you respond to this type of feedback? | Task-Level Feedback | Process-Level Feedback | Self-Regulation Level Feedback |
| **Step 4)** What observations might you see or hear that indicates a progression <u>away from</u> mastery? How will you respond to this type of feedback? | Task-Level Feedback | Process-Level Feedback | Self-Regulation Level Feedback |

# Exit Ticket

Take a moment and self-evaluate your learning in this module using these statements.

1.  I can identify the foundational components of feedback.

| 1 | 2 | 3 | 4 | 5 |
|---|---|---|---|---|
| Strongly disagree | Disagree | Neutral | Agree | Strongly agree |

Explain the reason for your selection.

_____

_____

2.  I can describe the three levels of feedback.

| 1 | 2 | 3 | 4 | 5 |
|---|---|---|---|---|
| Strongly disagree | Disagree | Neutral | Agree | Strongly agree |

Explain the reason for your selection.

_____

_____

3.  I can explain why it is important to respond to feedback and provide examples.

| 1 | 2 | 3 | 4 | 5 |
|---|---|---|---|---|
| Strongly disagree | Disagree | Neutral | Agree | Strongly agree |

Explain the reason for your selection.

_____

_____

# MODULE 15

# How Do I Develop Self-Regulated Mathematics Learners?

We arrive at this module with both a sense of relief and, hopefully, a sense of empowerment. Although this module is brief, we aim to bring this Playbook to a close. However, this closure is in page count only. Like an infinite sequence, asymptote, or recursive formula, the work simply cycles back to the starting point of this Playbook. As we sit down with our grade-level colleagues or our mathematics department, we review the pacing guide; identify the next standard, unit, or learning sequence; and start right back at Module #1. That's teaching.

However, our hope is that this journey, and the subsequent journeys through the Playbook, foster, nurture, and sustain self-regulated mathematics learners. Mathematics learners that:

- know their current level of conceptual knowledge and procedural fluency;

- know where they are going next in their mathematics learning;

- possess the capacity to drive their own learning through strategic competence;

- monitor their learning by applying their adaptive reasoning;

- recognize the productive dispositions necessary for successful mathematics learning;

- notice their thinking and learning and seek feedback about their mathematics progression; and

- acknowledge when they have developed proficiency in their conceptual knowledge and procedural fluency and support their peers in their own journey.

This journey was framed by three big ideas. Please record those big ideas one more time for emphasis.

1. _____

2. _____

3. _____

We are going to do something with these big ideas now as our final synthesis task for the Playbook.

Concept mapping is an evidence-generating strategy that shows relationships between ideas. In fact, you looked at effect size for concept mapping in Module #12. We would like for you to create a giant concept map of your learning in the Playbook.

Why would we do this? This Playbook is jammed full of ideas—complex teaching and learning ideas. And although the organization of this Playbook involves modules, the demarcation of modules is only for organizational purposes. Each module is tightly connected with the others. That is why we call this a "playbook." You may not move through this text in a linear sequence, but instead, you may move to the specific module that is most needed at the moment. A concept map of the ideas in this Playbook will help solidify the relationships and override the potential to silo the concepts into arbitrary modules. For example, analyzing the standards and evidence generation are strongly linked to Math Talk. Math Talk requires that we notice the content and quality of mathematics discussions in our classroom. However, we may have to scaffold those discussions for learners that need support in initiating and sustaining productive conversations. In addition, learners give, receive, and integrate feedback during conversations.

Do you see how it is all connected? Use the blank page to create a visual representation of the content, skills, and understandings in this Playbook. Use words, phrases, images, and colors. Pull in examples, nonexamples, and models from your classroom. Make this yours. When you are finished, step back, admire your work, and recognize that what is on that concept map is exactly how you will develop self-regulated learners in your mathematics classroom.

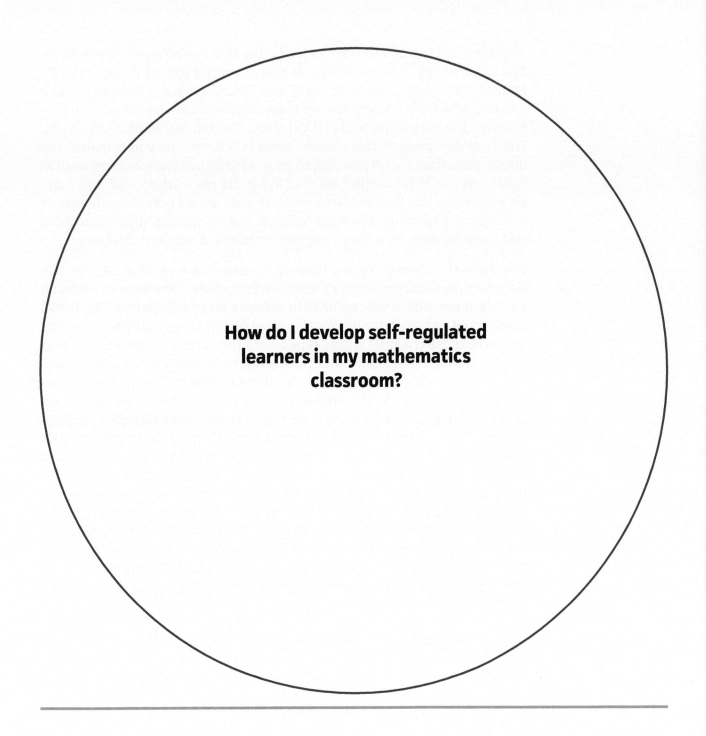

**How do I develop self-regulated learners in my mathematics classroom?**

In closing, we want to thank you for taking this learning journey with us. The opportunity to learn alongside you is something we do not take for granted. John, Kateri, Michelle, Doug, and Nancy recognize what an honor it is to be invited into you grade-level team, mathematics department, or professional learning community (PLC+) team. For that, we want to thank you. From our perspective, this collaboration is not over. As you translate the information from this Playbook into your school and classroom, we want to hear from you. What worked for you? What did not work so well? What are we missing in this goal of learning about what works best in mathematics teaching and learning? We want to know so that we can implement these ideas, approaches, strategies, and interventions in our own classrooms.

The very first words typed onto the screen of this Playbook in the Introduction asked you to pick a number. From there, you were led through a series of operations that resulted in arriving at the number 15. This initial task served as the metaphor for this Playbook. It is only fitting, then, that we make these the final words typed onto the screen. Regardless of your initial number, the specific numeric operations lead you to the final answer of 15. The numeric operations or decisions mathematically change your starting number to 15. Remember, regardless of the initial starting point of our learners, their encounters and experiences in our schools and classrooms have the potential to have a positive effect on their mathematics learning. They allow all learners the access and opportunity for successful mathematics learning. Just like the initial mathematics task in this module, these encounters and these experiences are purposeful, intentional, and deliberate. They are by design, not by chance. That is the power we have as mathematics teachers. That is the hope we have as mathematics educators. What happened over the course of the 15 modules of this Playbook, across the strategies and tasks of this Playbook, represents the decisions we make each and every day to ensure that our students have a great mathematics teacher, not by chance but by design.

Now, let's go teach some math!

# References

Alegre-Ansuategui, F. J., Moliner, L., Lorenzo, G., & Maroto, A. (2017). Peer tutoring and academic achievement in mathematics: A meta-analysis. *Eurasia Journal of Mathematics, Science and Technology Education, 14*, 337–354.

Almarode, J., Fisher, D., & Frey, N. (2023). *How feedback works: A playbook.* Corwin.

Antonetti, J., & Garver, J. (2015). *17,000 classroom visits can't be wrong.* ASCD.

Ball, D. L. (1993). With an eye toward the mathematical horizon: Dilemmas of teaching elementary school mathematics. *Elementary School Journal, 93,* 373–397.

Banse, H. W., Palacios, N. A., Merritt, E. G., & Rimm-Kaufman, S. E. (2016). 5 strategies for scaffolding math discourse with ELLs. *Teaching Children Mathematics, 23*(2), 100–108. https://doi .org/10.5951/teacchilmath.23.2.0100

Barbieri, C. A., Miller-Cotto, D., & Clerjuste, S. N. (2023). A meta-analysis of the worked examples effect on mathematics performance. *Educational Psychology, 35*(11), 1–33. https://doi.org/10.1007/ s10648-023-09745-1

Barlow, A. T., Gerstenschlager, N. E., Strayer, J. E., Lischka, A. E., Stephens, D. C., Hartland, K. S., & Willingham, J. C. (2018). Scaffolding for access to productive struggle. *Mathematics Teaching in the Middle School, 23*(4), 202–207. https://doi .org/10.5951/mathteacmiddscho.23.4.0202

Battista, M. (2017). *Mathematical reasoning and sense making: Reasoning and sense making in the mathematics classroom, grades 3-5* (pp. 1–22). National Council of Teachers of Mathematics.

Berliner, D. C. (1987). Simple views of effective teaching and a simple theory of classroom instruction. In D. Berliner & B. Rosenshine (Eds.), *Talks to teachers.* Random House.

Berliner, D. C. (1990). What's all the fuss about instructional time? In M. Ben-Peretz & R. Bromme (Eds.), *The nature of time in schools: Theoretical concepts, practitioner perceptions* (pp. 3–35). Teachers College Press.

Berry, III, R.Q., & Thunder, K. (2012). The promise of qualitative metasynthesis: Mathematics experiences of Black learners. *Journal of Mathematics Education at Teachers College, 3,* 43–55.

Blackburn, B. R. (2018). *Rigor is not a four-letter word.* Routledge.

Block, M. E. (1995). Use peer tutors and task sheets. *Strategies, 9*(4), 9–12.

Booth, J. L., Cooper, L., Donovan, M. S., Huyghe, A., Koedinger, K. R., & Paré-Blagoev, E. J. (2015). Design-based research within the constraints of practice: AlgebraByExample. *Journal of Education for Students Placed at Risk, 20*(1–2), 79–100.

Booth, J. L., Koedinger, K. R., & Paré-Blagoev, J. E. (2011). *Testing the worked example principle in real-world classrooms* [Paper presentation]. Biannual meeting of the Society for Research in Child Development, Montreal, Quebec, Canada.

Booth, J. L., Lange, K. E., Koedinger, K. R., & Newton, K. J. (2013). Using example problems to improve student learning in algebra: Differentiating between correct and incorrect examples. *Learning and Instruction, 25,* 24–34.

Carroll, C., Booth, J. L., & Davenport, J. (2016, November 1). *Teaching mathematics through student worked examples* [Webinar]. WestEd. https://www .wested.org/resources/teaching-mathematics-through-student-worked-examples

Carroll, W. M. (1994). Using worked examples as an instructional support in the algebra classroom. *Journal of Educational Psychology, 86*(3), 360–367.

Chapin, S. H., O'Connor, M. C., & Anderson, N. C. (2013). *Talk moves: A teacher's guide for using classroom discussions in math, grades K-6* (3rd ed.). Math Solutions.

Clark, E. (1997). *Designing and implementing an integrated curriculum: A student-centered approach.* Holistic Education Press.

Clark, R. C., Nguyen, F., & Sweller, J. (2011). *Efficiency in learning: Evidence-based guidelines to manage cognitive load.* John Wiley & Sons.

Dale, R., & Scherrer, J. (2015). Goldilocks discourse – Math scaffolding that's just right. *The Phi Delta Kappan, 97*(2), 58–61. http://www.jstor.org/ stable/24578377

Darwani, Zubainur, C. M., & Saminan. (2020). Adaptive reasoning and strategic competence through problem-based learning model in middle school. *Journal of Physics: Conference Series, 1460*(1), 012019.

Devos, N. J. (2015). *Peer interactions in new content and language-integrated settings.* Springer.

Dixon, J. (2018). *Providing scaffolding just in case.* http://www.dnamath.com/blog-post/five-ways-we-undermine-efforts-to-increase-student-achievement-and-what-to-do-about-it-part-3-of-5/

Englert, C. S., & Mariage, T. V. (1991). Making students partners in the comprehension process: Organizing the reading POSSE. *Learning Disability Quarterly, 14,* 123–138.

Ericsson, A., & Pool, R. (2016). *Peak: Secrets from the new science of expertise.* Houghton Mifflin Harcourt.

Fisher, D., & Frey, N. (2018). The uses and misuses of graphic organizers in content area learning. *The Reading Teacher, 71*(6), 763–766.

Fisher, D., Frey, N., Almarode, J., Flores, K., & Nagel, D. (2020). *PLC+: Better decisions and greater impact, by design.* Corwin.

Fisher, D., Frey, N., Ortega, S., & Hattie, J. (2023). *Teaching students to drive their learning: A playbook on engagement and self-regulation.* Corwin.

Fisher, D., Frey, N., Smith, D., & Hattie, J. (2021). *Rebound: A playbook for rebuilding agency, accelerating learning recovery, and rethinking schools.* Corwin.

Fredricks, J. A., Blumenfeld, P. C., & Paris, A. H. (2004). School engagement: Potential of the concept, state of the evidence. *Review of Educational Research, 74*(1), 59–109.

Frey, N., Fisher, D., & Almarode, J. T. (2023). *How scaffolding works: A playbook for supporting and releasing responsibility to students.* Corwin.

Frey, N., Shin, M., Fisher, D., & Biscocho, R. (2023). *Onboarding teachers: A playbook for getting new staff up to speed.* Corwin.

Fuchs, D., Fuchs, L., & Burish, P. (2000). Peer-assisted learning strategies: An evidence-based practice to promote reading achievement. *Learning Disabilities Research and Practice, 15*(2), 85–91.

Fuchs, L. S., Fuchs, D., & Kazdan, S. (1999). Effects of peer-assisted learning strategies on high school students with serious reading problems. *Remedial and Special Education, 20*(5), 309–318.

Furner, J. M., & Berman, B. T. (2012). Math anxiety: Overcoming a major obstacle to the improvement of student math performance. *Childhood Education, 79*(3). https://link.gale.com/apps/doc/A98467511/AONE?u=googlescholar&sid=bookmark-AONE&xid=181801e9

Georgia Department of Education. (2021). *Georgia K-12 mathematics standards.* https://www.gadoe.org/Curriculum-Instruction-and-Assessment/Curriculum-and-Instruction/Pages/GA-K12-Math-Standards.aspx

Goguen, J. (2005). What is a concept? Conceptual structures: Common semantics for sharing knowledge. *Lecture Notes in Computer Science, 3596,* 52–77. https://doi.org/10.1007/11524564_4

Gresham, G., & Shannon, T. (2017). Building mathematics discourse in students. *Teaching Children Mathematics, 23*(6), 360–366. https://doi.org/10.5951/teacchilmath.23.6.0360

Ha Dinh, T. T., Bonner, A., Clark, R., Ramsbotham, J., & Hines, S. (2016). The effectiveness of the teach-back method on adherence and self-management in health education for people with chronic disease: A systematic review. *JBI Database of Systematic Reviews and Implementation, 14*(1), 210–247.

Hastie, P. A., Rudisill, M. E., & Wadsworth, D. D. (2013). Providing students with voice and choice: Lessons from intervention research on autonomy-supportive climates in physical education. *Sport, Education & Society, 18*(1), 38–56.

Hattie, J. (2023). *Visible learning: The sequel: A synthesis of over 2100 meta-analyses relating to achievement.* Routledge.

Henningsen, M., & Stein, M. K. (1997). Mathematical tasks and student cognition: Classroom-based factors that support and inhibit high-level mathematical thinking and reasoning. *Journal for Research in Mathematics Education, 28,* 524–549.

Hiebert, J. S., & Grouws, D. A. (2007). The effects of classroom mathematics teaching on students' learning. In F. K. Lester Jr., (Ed.), *Second handbook of research on mathematics teaching and learning* (pp. 371–404). Information Age Publishing.

Hufferd-Ackles, K., Fuson, K. C., & Sherin, M. G. (2004). Describing levels and components of a math-talk learning community. *Journal for Research in Mathematics Education, 35,* 81–116.

Jacobson, J., Thrope, L., Fisher, D., Lapp, D., Frey, N., & Flood, J. (2001). Cross-age tutoring: A literacy improvement approach for struggling adolescent readers. *Journal of Adolescent and Adult Literacy, 44,* 528–536.

Kahneman, D. (2011). *Thinking fast and slow.* Farrar, Straus and Giroux.

Kalinec-Craig, C. A. (2017). The rights of the learner: A framework for promoting equity through formative assessment in mathematics education. *Democracy and Education, 25* (2), Article 5. https://democracyeducationjournal.org/home/vol25/iss2/5

Kapur, M. (2016). Examining productive failure, productive success, unproductive failure, and unproductive success in learning. *Educational Psychologist, 51*(2), 289–299.

Kapur, M. (2019, September 28). *Productive failure.* Tedx Lugano. https://www.manukapur.com/prof-manu-kapur-at-tedx-lugano-sep-28-2019/

Korteling, J. E., & Toet, A. (2022). Cognitive biases. In S. Della Sala (Ed.), *Encyclopedia of behavioural neuroscience* (2nd ed., pp. 610–619). Elsevier.

Lange, K. E., Booth, J. L., & Newton, K. J. (2014). Learning algebra from worked examples. *The Mathematics Teacher, 107*(7), 534–540. https://doi.org/10.5951/mathteacher.107.7.0534

Maheady, L., Harper, G. F., & Mallette, B. (2001). Peer-mediated instruction and interventions and students with mild disabilities. *Remedial and Special Education, 22*, 4–15.

McNeil, L. (2012). Using talk to scaffold referential questions for English language learners. *Teaching and Teacher Education, 28*(3), 396–404.

Merriam-Webster. (2023). Playbook. https://www.merriam-webster.com/dictionary/playbook

Meyer, D. K., & Turner, J. C. (2007). Scaffolding emotions in classrooms. In P. A. Schutz & R. Pekrun (Eds.), *Emotion in education* (pp. 243–258). Elsevier Academic Press.

Muin, A., Hanifah, S. H., & Diwidian, F. (2018). The effect of creative problem solving on students' mathematical adaptive reasoning. *Journal of Physics: Conference Series, 948*, 012001.

National Council of Teachers of Mathematics (NCTM). (2014). *Principles to actions: Ensuring mathematical success for all*. NCTM.

National Council of Teachers of Mathematics (NCTM). (2020a). *Catalyzing change in early childhood and elementary mathematics: Initiating critical conversations*. NCTM.

National Council of Teachers of Mathematics (NCTM). (2020b). *Catalyzing change in middle school mathematics: Initiating critical conversations*. NCTM.

National Council of Teachers of Mathematics (NCTM). (2020c). *Catalyzing change in high school mathematics: Initiating critical conversations*. NCTM.

National Council of Teachers of Mathematics (NCTM). (n.d.). *Access and equity in mathematics education*. https://www.nctm.org/Standards-and-Positions/Position-Statements/Access-and-Equity-in-Mathematics-Education/

National Council of Teachers of Mathematics (NCTM). (n.d.). *Principles and standards for school mathematics*. https://www.nctm.org/Standards-and-Positions/Principles-and-Standards/Process/

National Research Council. (2001). Adding it up: Helping children learn mathematics. In J. Kilpatrick., J. Swafford, & B. Findell (Eds.), *Mathematics learning study committee, center for education, division of behavioral and social sciences and education*. National Academy Press.

O'Connor, M. C., & Michaels, S. (1993). Aligning academic task and participation status through revoicing: Analysis of a classroom discourse strategy. *Anthropology & Education Quarterly, 24*(4), 318–335. https://doi.org/10.1525/aeq.1993.24.4.04x0063k

Posner, G. J. (2004). *Analyzing the curriculum* (3rd ed.). McGraw Hill.

Rawding, M. R., & Wills, T. (2012). Discourse: Simple moves that work. *Mathematics Teaching in the Middle School, 18*, 46–51.

Rickards, F., Hattie, J., & Reid, C. (2021). *The turning point for the teaching profession. Growing expertise and evaluative thinking*. Routledge.

Rosenthal, R., & Jacobson, L. (1968). Pygmalion in the classroom. *The Urban Review, 3*(1), 16–20.

Rosenthal, R., & Jacobson, L. (1992). *Pygmalion in the classroom: Teacher expectation and pupils' intellectual development* (Newly expanded ed.). Crown House.

Schoenfeld, A. H. (2011). Noticing matters. A lot. Now what? In M. G. Sherin, V. R. Jacobs, & R. A. Philipp (Eds.), *Mathematics teacher noticing: Seeing through the teachers' eyes* (pp. 3–13). Routledge.

Sherin, M. G., Jacobs, V. R., & Philipp, R. A. (2011). Situating the study of teacher noticing. In M. G. Sherin, V. R. Jacobs, & R. A. Philipp (Eds.), *Mathematics teacher noticing: Seeing through the teachers' eyes* (pp. 3–13). Routledge.

Skemp, R. R. (1976). Relational understanding and instrumental understanding. *Mathematics Teaching, 77*, 20–26.

Smith, M. S., Hughes, E. K., Engle, R. A., & Stein, M. K. (2009). Orchestrating discussions. *Mathematics Teaching in the Middle School, 14*, 548–556.

Sweller, J., & Cooper, G. A. (1985). The use of worked examples as a substitute for problem solving in learning algebra. *Cognition and Instruction, 2*(1), 59–89. http://www.jstor.org/stable/3233555

Texas Education Agency. (2015). *Texas essential knowledge and skills for mathematics*.

Tjeerdsma, B. L. (1995). How to motivate students . . . without standing on your head! *Journal of Physical Education, Recreation, and Dance, 66*(5), 36–39.

Virginia Board of Education. (2016). *Mathematics standards of learning for Virginia Public Schools, K–12*.

Vrabie, D. (2021). *The three forms of feedback: Appreciation, coaching, and evaluation*. CTO Craft. https://ctocraft.com/blog/the-three-forms-of-feedback-appreciation-coaching-and-evaluation/

Vygotsky, L. (1978). *Mind in society: The development of higher psychological processes* (M. Cole, V. John-Steiner, S. Scribner, & E. Souberman, Eds.). Harvard University Press.

Wagganer, E. L. (2015). Creating math talk communities. *Teaching Children Mathematics, 22*(4), 248–254. https://doi.org/10.5951/teacchilmath.22.4.0248

Walter, H. A. (2018). Beyond turn and talk: Creating discourse. *Teaching Children Mathematics, 25*(3), 180–185. https://doi.org/10.5951/teacchilmath.25.3.0180

Wang, M.-T., Fredricks, J., Ye, F., Hofkens, T., & Linn, J. S. (2019). Conceptualization and assessment of adolescents' engagement and disengagement in school: A multidimensional school engagement scale. *European Journal of Psychological Assessment, 35*(4), 592–606. https://doi.org/10.1027/1015-5759/a000431

Warshauer, H. K. (2015). Strategies to support productive struggle. *Mathematics Teaching in the Middle School, 20*(7), 390–393. https://doi.org/10.5951/mathteacmiddscho.20.7.0390

Wiggins, G. (2012). Seven keys to effective feedback. *Educational Leadership, 70*(1), 10–16.

Witzel, B. S., & Little, M. E. (2016). *Teaching elementary mathematics to struggling learners.* The Guilford Press.

Wood, D., Bruner, J. S., & Ross, G. (1976). The role of tutoring in problem solving. *Journal of Child Psychology and Psychiatry, 17*(2), 89–100.

Yale University. (2022). RULER approach. Yale Center for Emotional Intelligence. https://www.rulerapproach.org/

Zwiers, J., O'Hara, S., & Pritchard, R. (2014). *Common core standards in diverse classrooms: Essential practices for developing academic language and disciplinary literacy.* Stenhouse.

# Index

# Keep learning...

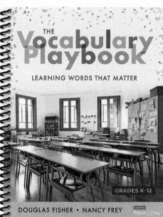
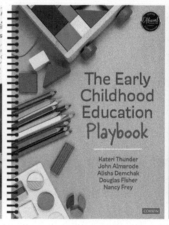
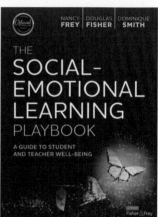

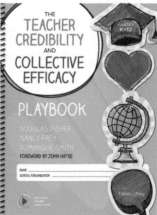

**Helping educators make the greatest impact**

**CORWIN HAS ONE MISSION:** to enhance education through intentional professional learning.

We build long-term relationships with our authors, educators, clients, and associations who partner with us to develop and continuously improve the best evidence-based practices that establish and support lifelong learning.